WALKING IN CLYDESDALE

Paul Lamarra

Tinto Press

NB. A compass is required for the following routes:-

p.61 Culter Fell from Culter Allers (Birthwood)

p. 101 Rome Hill and Tewsgill Hill

Published by Tinto Press, PO Box 9420, Lanark, ML11 7QL

British Library Cataloguing in Publication Data
A CIP record for this book is available from the British Library.

ISBN: 0 95422 850 2

Typesetting & Design by: Iwik Designs

Cover Design: Iwik Designs

Photographs: Paul Lamarra

Cover Photographs: Main cover picture - walking in Cowgill Glen; bottom left -Tinto Hill from the Hartree Hills; bottom right - the River Clyde.

Maps: Jeremy Semmens

Printed by: CCB Print, Glasgow

Disclaimer: the information in this book is given in good faith and is believed to be correct at the time of publication. No responsibility is accepted by either the author or the publisher for errors or omissions, or for any loss or injury howsoever caused. Only you can judge your own fitness, competence and experience.

PREFACE

The intention of this book is to refocus attention on Clydesdale as a walking destination. There are many guidebooks to surrounding areas that have included one or two of the better known walks from Clydesdale and the result has been that many pleasurable walks have been forgotten.

Walking in Clydesdale isn't an end in itself as there is so much to discover as you walk. It is the perfect destination for those who want relatively gentle and interesting walks that are close to towns and amenities such as pubs serving good beer and good food to round off the day's walking. For those seeking solitude and a strenuous day's walking there is plenty on offer around Culter Fell and in the Lowther Hills.

Hopefully through this book Clydesdale will once again be regarded as a credible walking destination and Biggar, Lanark or Leadhills as a place around which to base a walking holiday.

I would like to thank the following for their generous assistance: Simon Pilpel, John Gavin, Richard Carmichael of Carmichael, Andy Nelson, Vincent Lunny, Stewart Love, Helen, Colin and Lucy Thomson, Richard Scott, Larry O'Hare, Claire Loughran, May Lamarra, Karen Gillon MSP and Ed Archer. Very special thanks to Hugh Murray for always being ready to turn up, to John Lamarra and Donald Lamont for their meticulous proof reading and Catherine, Beth and Claire for their patience.

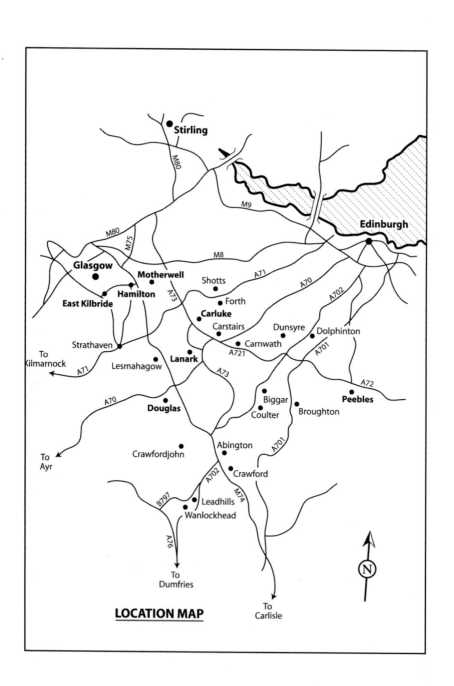

LOCATION MAP

CONTENTS

Looking out over the Clyde Valley from Tinto Hill

INTRODUCTION

USING THE GUIDE

Of the 40 or so walks in this guide most are circular and described in the direction, which I found through experience, derives the greatest benefit from the weather and the terrain.

The walks are arranged according to the closest town or village. For each village there is a historical background, travel directions, details of public transport, where to eat and where to stay. For some routes the directions for travel to the start of the route are given separately at the start of the route description in *Essential Facts*.

The Essential Facts details the length of the route, the difficulty of the route and a brief description of the terrain so that you can decide on each route's suitability. It will also tell you the maps required and whether you need a compass or not.

By the Way is a commentary on each route. It provides information on things to look out for and historical contexts although sometimes it provides no more than an excuse to try the walk. This is followed by a detailed breakdown of distances and directions with Ordnance Survey grid references. The simple maps are is some cases adequate but mostly they are for the purpose of picking out the route on the OS maps. Ideally, read *By the Way* at your leisure and take a copy of the detailed directions with you suitably protected from the elements.

A BRIEF HISTORY OF CLYDESDALE

Clydesdale is generally taken to be the southern part of Lanarkshire that has the Clyde watershed as its boundary. In stark contrast to industrial Lanarkshire further to the north, it is an area of outstanding natural beauty comprised of extensive moors, rolling hills and classic farmland.

The Southern Upland Boundary Fault which runs across Clydesdale from Crawfordjohn to Biggar, separates the gentle lowlands cut into by the Clyde and its tributaries from the high rolling hills of the Southern Uplands with their wide glaciated valleys. It is often assumed that Tinto Hill, Lanarkshire's best known and best loved landmark, is the most northerly outlier of the Southern Uplands but rather it is an igneous extrusion that stands alone to the north of the fault.

It is clear that Clydesdale has been a choice place to live for thousands of years as it had on offer the irresistible combination of fertile land by the Clyde and many small isolated hillocks close by that were ideal for the building of necessarily defensive settlements.

Human occupation began about 8000 years ago with the arrival of the Mesolithic (middle stone age) people, evidence of whom has been found in the form of stone tools by the banks of the Clyde near Crawford. Later Neolithic settlers left a more definitive stamp by building settlements and starting the process of clearing woodland that leaves the largely treeless landscape we see today. Only inaccessible pockets of this ancient woodland remain today notably in the steep sided Mouse (locally known as the moose) and Nethan Valleys.

Some of the most conspicuous evidence of early human presence on the landscape dates from the Bronze Age and the most striking example is the huge cairn that surmounts Tinto Hill. The Iron Age people who followed were the most prodigious fort and settlement builders exploiting the hilltops and the discrete valleys. The remains of their distinctive circular forts with double ramparts are to be found all over Clydesdale. One of the easiest to detect is on the lower slopes of Tinto Hill at Fallburn.

The Iron Age ceased with the arrival of the Romans. The Romans came in three waves, once under the orders of Flavian in AD110 and twice under Antonine between AD139 and AD161. The Romans attempted and failed to quell the northern tribes on each of these occasions but they built many forts and camps and the roads to link them. The biggest fort was at Castledykes to the east of Lanark near Ravenstruther.

Constantine legalised Christianity and although the Romans had departed, southern Scotland still fell under this influence. St Ninian famously converted the Picts. St Ninian's well and chapel at Lamington and the ancient chapel at Warrenhill, hint at the presence of his fifth-century mission in Clydesdale. St Kentigern followed up St Ninian's good work and he may have been based in Broughton for a time, possibly baptising local resident Merlin.

David I patronised the anglicised Normans and Flemings giving them land in return for their support; he also introduced the feudal system of government. The Lords were given the right to raise taxes from tenants - who in turn would expect protection - appoint a priest and try criminals. Culter Motte Hill is a good example of the Norman brand of settlement and can be visited with a short detour from the Biggar- Langlees walk.

As trade developed with Europe in the 12th century the King granted charters to create Royal Burghs. The charter allowed the burgh to hold weekly markets and a number of fairs each year. Lanark is one of the oldest of the 66 Royal Burghs in Scotland, receiving its charter in 1140. Royal Burghs couldn't deal with the burgeoning trade, so trading privileges were widened to burghs of barony. Charters were granted to local barons but foreign goods had to be purchased from a Royal Burgh. There were many burghs of barony created in Clydesdale including Biggar and Carnwath in the 15th century and Carluke and Lesmahagow in the 17th century. Burghs of Barony such as Crawfordjohn and Roberton failed to attract much trade and remain tiny hamlets. Rich in resources, the 18th and 19th centuries saw Clydesdale playing a prominent part in the Industrial Revolution. Mining for lead and coal was stepped up, the Clyde was harnessed to power the mills built by David Dale and Richard Arkwright, the Wilson brothers opened their cutting edge iron works at Wilsontown near Forth and the shale oil industry thrived at Tarbrax. All of these activities had a major impact on the surrounding landscapes. New communities with new values were created in places where people were unaccustomed to living, railways reached into almost every corner and spoil heaps of every shade now dot the countryside. Despite being feted for the forward and altruistic thinking that accompanied industrial development in Clydesdale, industry died a slow death. Today, industrial heritage and tourism along with agriculture are Clydesdale's mainstays.

THE KILLING TIMES, 1662 -1668

Greenhill Covenanter's Museum, Biggar

A feature of the Clydesdale countryside is the number of memorials to Covenanters who were executed for their beliefs. They fought to be free of patronage and government interference in their religion and set out to establish Presbyterianism throughout Britain and Ireland.

The high lonely moors were popular spots for the gathering of Covenanters to worship God and to hear their *outed* ministers preach. These gatherings were known as conventicles. Conventicles were sought out and ruthlessly put down by the government. The need to hold conventicles arose from Charles II's wish to impose bishops and patronage on the Presbyterian Church of Scotland in 1662.

In 1638 many ministers of the Church of Scotland and noblemen had signed the *National Covenant* and again in 1643 the *Solemn League and Covenant* with the English Parliamentarians hence Covenanters. The Covenant of 1638 was in response to Charles I and Bishop Laud's desire to impose a new prayer book - Laud's Liturgy - and episcopacy on the Presbyterian Church. Through signing the Covenant the signatories pledged themselves to maintain the true religion free of patronage. These events precipitated the Bishops' Wars of 1639 - 41.

In 1662, those who supported the covenants did not take too kindly to yet another attempt by a Stuart king to control the Church of Scotland. Therefore, 270 of the ministers who were obliged to resign and apply to Charles II's bishops to be reappointed refused and undertook open-air worship in defiance. These were the *outed* ministers. A 1665 act banned conventicles under pain of fine, imprisonment or corporal punishment. The Pentland Rising followed in 1666 but the Covenanters were defeated at Rullion Green.

Two attempts at reconciliation attracted some ministers back to their parishes but those who still refused suffered even harsher repression which only strengthened their cause and resolve. By 1678 south-west Scotland in particular was outwith government control and so the Highland Host, nearly 10 000 Highland and Lowland troops were sent in to maintain order. The heavy handed approach made revolt even more likely and in June 1679 an armed conventicle defeated government troops under the command of James Graham of Claverhouse at Drumclog. Buoyed by this victory 4000 Covenanters gathered on the banks of the Clyde at Hamilton three weeks later. Success was short lived as the Covenanters were heavily defeated by the forces of the Duke of Monmouth in battle at Bothwell Bridge.

The Duke of Monmouth initiated a third attempt at reconciliation but some still refused to submit and organised themselves into a group known as the Cameronians which were under the command of hard line Covenanters Richard Cameron and Donald Cargill.

Cameron and Cargill were behind the Declaration of Sanquhar of 1680 denouncing their allegiance to the King. One month after the declaration, the Cameronians were defeated at Aird's Moss in Ayrshire and Cameron was killed. Cargill was captured near Thankerton and hanged in Edinburgh in 1681. James VII, who came to the throne in 1685 allowed Presbyterians to worship in their own way but he did not extend an amnesty to the Cameronians. James Renwick, a Cameronian minister was the last to be executed in 1688.

1690 saw William and Mary of Orange on the throne and parliamentary approval for the Presbyterian form of church government but the Covenants of 1638 and 1641 which pledged to establish Presbyterianism throughout Britain and Ireland were ignored. The Cameronians continued to support the Covenant and in 1712 their minister John McMillan renewed the Covenants on Auchensaugh Moor (between Douglas and Crawfordjohn). Despite also excommunicating Queen Anne and her parliament, the events went largely unnoticed.

PREPARATION FOR THE HILLS
Most of the walks in this guide do not require any special preparation - just an awareness of what the most appropriate clothing and footwear might be. If you are heading into the hills you should have the necessary knowledge, experience and equipment to deal with severe weather and challenging navigation. In the description of the routes in hill country it has been assumed that the walker has the required technical skill.

A WORD ABOUT NAVIGATING
For many of the walks the maps and directions contained in this book will suffice. However for walks on the open moors and in the hills, where landmarks and distinguishing features are rare, a more detailed map is essential as is a compass.

The Ordnance Survey produces two series of maps that are useful to walkers. The Landranger series is drawn to a scale of 1:50000. Landranger maps cover a large area and are of adequate detail, although some footpaths may not be included.

The Explorer series is drawn to a scale of 1: 25 000. Explorer maps cover a much smaller area than the Landranger maps and can sometimes provide bewildering detail. Explorer maps do require more skill to read but they do include many more place names than the Landranger maps and can give the walker a greater feel for the landscape, the people who have lived in it and the area's history. In a few places several maps of one type overlap or come together - in these cases there is a recommended map in the *Essential Facts*.

It would be unwise to attempt any of the walks in the hills unless you are comfortable fixing and following a bearing. On the one or two occasions where a bearing is given in the guide it is a magnetic bearing.

DONALDS
There are no Munros (mountains over 3000 feet) or Corbett's (hills over 2 500 feet) in Clydesdale. There are however 21of the 87 Donalds in Clydesdale or shared with neighbouring counties. *The Donalds*, is the list compiled by Percy Donald, of all the hills in the south of Scotland of hills over 2000 feet that have 100 feet of re-ascent on all sides.

Not all of the 21 Donalds are covered by this guide but here is a list of the ones that are: Tinto Hill, Culter Fell, Cardon Hill, Chapelgill Fell, Wedder Law, Scaw'd Law, Ballenceluch Law, Rodger Law, Lowther Hill, Green Lowther, Cold Moss, Dun Law and Lousie Wood Law.

ACCESS

Many of the walks outlined in this book do follow rights of way and those are highlighted but it should not be assumed that because a walk is included a right of way exists. It is also the case that the Ordnance Survey maps do not distinguish rights of way from other paths. However Scotland has always had a strong tradition of access especially to open country and new rights of public access to the outdoors, conditional on responsible behaviour, have now been enshrined in the Land Reform (Scotland) Act 2003 but do not come into effect until sometime in 2004. How to take and manage access responsibly will be set out in the forthcoming *Scottish Outdoor Access* code, but at the time of going to print this is still being developed. I have therefore reproduced advice for walkers previously published on behalf of the Access Forum and would encourage users of the guide to follow this interim advice.

A CODE FOR WALKERS AND VISITORS TO SCOTLAND'S HILLS AND MOUNTAINS

Approach to the hills

The approach to the hills is often through enclosed land and settlements. This land is used intensively and so visitors need to take particular care to choose sensible routes.

- Make use of public transport and share cars where possible to minimise congestion and protect the environment.
- If going by car, park safely off road and do not block tracks or gateways.

If possible, when passing through enclosed land and woodland:

- Walk along tracks, paths or field edges.
- Use gates and stiles, leaving gates as you find them.
- Avoid damage to any fences or dykes that have to be crossed.

Respect the needs and privacy of those who live and work in the countryside.

Care for the hills

The hills have a great attraction for walkers and they contain important and sensitive habitats and wildlife. You can help conserve it by:

- Avoiding disturbance or damage to animals, birds, trees and plants.
- Minimising erosion. Avoid widening paths, cutting corners on zigzags and running downhill.
- Removing all litter and food scraps.
- Refraining from building new cairns or leaving waymarks.
- Burying excrement well away from paths or watercourses and not polluting streams or lochs.

Consider others on the hill

Enjoy the peace and solitude of the hills.

- Avoid making unnecessary noise.
- Keep groups small and act unobtrusively.
- If you come across equipment leave it. Others may depend on it for work or safety.

Make sure you are properly equipped and have the skills and fitness necessary for what you want to do in the hills.

Land Management

The land is a place of work for many, such as farmers or keepers, who depend on it for their livelihood and are responsible for its management.

- Avoid disturbing farm animals.
- Keep dogs on a lead when crossing enclosed land or on the hill during the breeding season. Avoid taking dogs into fields with livestock.

Some times of the year are particularly sensitive:

- Avoid sheep just before and during the lambing season (March to May).
- If you come across deer calves, leave them alone.

Before setting out for the hills during the stalking season (critical period mid-August to mid-October) make local enquiries through the local tourist office or phone one of the numbers listed below.

STALKING AND SHOOTING

The deer stalking season can start as early as July and continue through to the end of February. The grouse shooting season begins on 12th August and continues on some estates until January. For your own safety and to safeguard the livelihoods of all those involved in shooting it is essential that you do not disturb a shoot. If you intend walking in the hills especially in the Pentlands, the Lowthers and around Culter Fell then it is best to make enquiries locally. Listed below are some of the estates who conduct shoots in Clydesdale.

Culter Fell
Mr G. McCosh,
Estate Office, Culter Allers ~ (01899) 220410

Pentland Hills
Lee &Carnwath Estates, Main St, Carnwath ~ (01555) 840273

Douglas
Douglas & Angus Estates, Newmains, Douglas ~ (01555) 851536

The Lowther Hills
Buccleuch Countryside Services ~ (01848) 331555.

TOURIST INFORMATION CENTRES AND OTHER USEFUL CONTACTS

Abington TIC,

Welcome Break,

Motorway Service Area (Junction 13, M74) Abington ML12 6R.

(01864) 502436; abington@seeglasgow.com

Biggar TIC,

155 High Street, Biggar, ML12 6DL,

(01899) 221066; biggar@seeglasgow.com

Glasgow TIC,

11 George Square, Glasgow, G2 1DY

(0141) 204 4400; enquiries@seeglasgow.com

Hamilton TIC,

Road Chef Services, (M74 Northbound), Hamilton ML3 6JW,

(01698) 285590; hamilton@seeglasgow.com

Lanark TIC,

Horsemarket, Ladyacre Road, Lanark, ML11 7LQ, (01555) 661661; lanark@seeglasgow.com

Scottish Wildlife Trust,

SWT Visitor Centre,

The Falls of Clyde Nature Reserve,

New Lanark, ML11 9DB ~ (01555) 665262, www.swt.org.uk

New Lanark World Heritage Site,

New Lanark Mills, New Lanark ~ (01555) 661345, www.newlanark.org

Clyde Valley Woodlands LIFE Project,

www.clydevalleywoods.org.uk

Scottish Natural Heritage,

Battleby, Redgorton, Perth, PH1 3EW, (01738) 444177

THE LANARK AND NEW LANARK
(WITH LISTINGS FOR KIRKFIELDBANK)
ROUTES

Lanark

Lanark is an intimate market town that sits high above the Clyde on a classic defensive site, and it can trace its history back to Roman times. Elevated to a Royal Burgh in 1140 by David I, Lanark entered its hey day. Lanark was en route for Kings wishing to visit the south west of their kingdom or the upper Tweed valley. William I and Alexander II were frequent visitors and Robert the Bruce was the patron of a Franciscan Friary where the Clydesdale Inn stands today. It was in 1183 that Pope Lucius III made reference to the town's school Lanark Grammar in a Papal Bull making it one of the oldest schools in Britain.

The claim to fame that Lanark prefers is that William Wallace is reputed to have wooed his wife Marion Braidfute in Lanark, having met her at the town's St. Kentigern's Church, the ruin of which can be found in the cemetery at the junction of Ladyacre Road and Hyndford Road.

After a street skirmish involving Wallace and some English soldiers garrisoned in Lanark, Edward I's sheriff executed Marion, instead of her husband Wallace who had fled the scene. Wallace avenged her death by killing Heselrig and thus set himself on the path to rebellion against English occupation and becoming the hero of the Wars of Independence. A statue of the stocky Wallace is incorporated into the clock tower of St. Nicholas Church at the foot of High Street and a plaque opposite marks the likely spot of his Lanark home.

The medieval town was centred on the area around St Nicholas Church known as the Castlegate and the Bloomgate. The oldest buildings are marked out by their crow-stepped gables. The High Street although mainly

St Nicholas Church, Lanark

Victorian is nevertheless built on the medieval pattern of burghage plots - long narrow strips of land extending back from a High St frontage. The building that protrudes from the line of buildings at the foot of the High Street is the 18th century Tollbooth which would have housed the town's courtroom and gaol.

A book detailing three heritage walks is available from the Tourist Information Centre (just along from the railway station and bus station). The walks take in the buildings of note in the medieval town and the impressive Hope Street.

NEW LANARK

These days it is New Lanark, Lanark's precocious offspring, that gets all the attention and deservedly so. A perfectly preserved 18th century factory village in a stunning woodland setting by the River Clyde it has been designated a World Heritage Site by UNESCO. World Heritage Site status was also awarded for the radical programme of social improvement which brought the village to particular prominence.

The New Lanark UNESCO World Heritage site.

New Lanark began as a project initiated by Richard Arkwright and David Dale. Arkwright believed that New Lanark would become the Manchester of Scotland and by 1799 four mills were operational, employing 2000 people who were housed in the specially built tenement rows.

Robert Owen took over the running of the mills from his father-in-law David Dale and it was he who enthusiastically pursued the village's radical programme of social improvement. Not only were the mill workers and their families comparatively well housed but they were also provided with evening lectures, schooling and nursery care and a co-operative store which was to serve as the prototype for the co-operative movement.

New Lanark went into decline after the mills closed in 1968 and demolition was contemplated but thanks to an enthusiastic housing association and the New Lanark Conservation Trust it is a thriving community and visitor attraction.

Most of the tenements are now occupied. A large part of one row has been converted to an excellent youth hostel, there are the 'see-it-as-it-was' attractions, one of the mills has been converted to a first class hotel and there are a number of speciality shops. The Scottish Wildlife Trust has a base and a visitor centre from where they manage the Falls of Clyde Nature Reserve.

GETTING THERE

Road

From Glasgow: leave the M74 at junction 7, Larkhall and follow the A72, Clyde Valley Tourist Route for 12 miles to Lanark. From the south: leave the M74 at junction 12 and then follow the A70 east and over the Hyndford Bridge into Lanark. From Edinburgh: leave the M8 at junction 6, Newhouse, signed for Lanark and Airdrie and follow the A73 for 15 miles west via Newmains and Carluke. Alternatively follow the A70 west out of Edinburgh, signed for Ayr and Kilmarnock via Juniper Green, Balerno to Carnwath. Follow the A70 through Carstairs Village to take up the A743 at Ravenstruther into Lanark. Journey times: Glasgow/Edinburgh to Lanark, 45 minutes - 1 hour.

For New Lanark follow directions for Lanark then once in Lanark follow signs for New Lanark.

Rail

There are two trains an hour linking Lanark with Glasgow, Monday to Saturday. Times of arrival/departure differ on a Saturday. On Sunday the service is hourly. Journey time: Glasgow to Lanark - 1 hour. This service is operated by Scotrail.

Bus

McKindless Group operates a service every 15 minutes, Monday to Saturday, from Hamilton to Lanark via Motherwell - service 41. Journey time: Hamilton to Lanark - 50 minutes. There is also an hourly service operated by HAD Coaches from Hamilton to Lanark via the Clyde Valley. Journey Time: Hamilton to Lanark - 45 minutes.

For all public transport enquiries call Traveline 0870 608 2 608.

EATING AND DRINKING

Lanark (01555 -)

Armando's Chip Shop & Restaurant, 90 High Street ~ 663797
Brewer's Fayre, Lanark Loch, 170 Hyndford Road ~ 663638
The Courtyard Restaurant, 3 Castlegate ~ 663900
The Clydesdale Inn, 15 Bloomgate ~ 663455
The Crown Tavern, 17 Hope Street ~ 664639
Daisies Coffee Shop, 18-22 Broomgate ~ 665209
East India Company, Indian Restaurant, 32 Wellgate ~ 663827
Harlequin Coffee Shop, Wide Close ~ 664000
The Horse & Jockey (Bar), 56 High Street ~ 662824
The Market Restaurant, Hyndford Road ~ 663658

The Original Tearoom, 32 Bannatyne Street ~ 664962
Prego Italian Restaurant, 3 High Street ~ 666300
Ristorante La Vigna, 40 Wellgate ~ 664320
Valerio's Fish & chicken Bar, Bannatyne Street ~ 665818
The Wallace Cave Bar, 11 Bloomgate, 663662
Woodpecker Restaurant & Bar, 20 Wide Close ~ 665161

New Lanark (01555 -)
New Lanark Mill Hotel, Mill One ~ 667200; there is also a cafeteria attached to the New Lanark
Visitor Attraction.

Kirkfieldbank (01555-)
Lovejoys Restaurant, 203 Riverside Road ~ 666277
Kirkfiedbank Tavern, 200 Riverside Road ~ 662537

STAYING
Lanark (01555 -)
Cartland Bridge Hotel, Glasgow Road ~ 664426
Bankhead Farm, Braxfield Road ~ 666560
Duneaton, 159 Hyndford Road ~ 665487
Jerviswood Mains Farm, Cleghorn Road ~ 663987
The Mains, 2 Muir Glen ~ 660219
St Catherine's B&B, 1 Kenilworth Road ~ 662295
Summerlea, 32 Hyndford Road ~ 664889

New Lanark (01555 -)
New Lanark Mill Hotel, Mill One ~ 667200
New Lanark Youth Hostel, Wee Row, Rosedale Street ~ 666710

Kirkfieldbank (01555-)
Brig End B&B, 231 Riverside Road ~ 663855
Corehouse Farm ~ 661377
Clarkston Farm ~ 663751
Clyde Valley Caravan Park ~ 663951

OUTDOOR EQUIPMENT STORE
Frasers of Lanark,
2 Bannatyne Street, Lanark ~ (01555) 665606

NEW LANARK AND THE FALLS OF CLYDE

Distance: 8 miles circular.

Grade: moderate.

Starting/finishing Point: New Lanark Visitor Centre.

Maps: OS Landranger 72, OS Explorer 335. Compass not required.

Terrain: the route follows well defined paths. There is a short moderate climb to the Corra Linn viewpoint and a longer moderate climb from Kirkfieldbank to Castlebank Park.

BY THE WAY

It is fitting that this should be the first walk in this book for it is one of the best riverside walks in the country. It is also a walk for all seasons and for all abilities. In the spring you can look in on the nesting peregrines and the canopy of trees either keeps you pleasantly cool or takes the edge off wild weather while providing a fine autumnal display. In winter it is the River Clyde surging through the deep gorge and over falls that will intimidate and hypnotise.

To walk from New Lanark upstream is to follow in the footsteps of the crowned heads of Europe, poets, writers and artists who not only came to see the New Lanark way of doing things but to marvel at the Corra Linn - the largest of the series of four falls that is known as the Falls of Clyde. A smaller set of falls is passed as you leave New Lanark and is known as the Dundaff Linn.

When the river is in spate you should be able to hear it thundering over the Corra Linn above the humming turbines of the hydro-electric power station and it is just beyond the power station that you will begin the climb to an excellent vantage point from which to view the Clyde dropping into a huge sandstone cauldron. Detouring to the highest level you will encounter an old pavilion that was once lined by mirrors so that the person inside felt as though they were at the centre of the falls.

From this point on the Clyde flows far below the path in a narrow rocky gorge although when the river is in spate it can feel very close. It is on the cliffs lining the river that a pair of peregrine falcons has chosen to nest. In the spring you will be asked in advance of reaching this point to be as quiet as possible and the gorge will be screened from view. There is usually a warden on hand to fill you in on the chicks' development and let you peer into the nest on the far side of the river with the aid of binoculars.

Continuing upstream it is not long before you will encounter the Bonnington Linn the furthest upstream of the Falls of Clyde and although smaller than the Corra Linn they can at times seem more ferocious as they are split by islands and great spikes of rock. The best view of the falls is from the far side of the river and just a little further upstream the river can be crossed at the weir. The weir diverts water into the hydro-electric power station and so inevitably reduces the impact of the falls, however on a few days of the year the weir is raised out of the way so that the falls can be seen in all their glory.

The walk downstream can be conducted right by the edge of the gorge where extreme care should be taken. The path by the edge of the gorge should be avoided when the peregrines are nesting by following the broad path a hundred yards or so from the river. Either way it is a very pleasant woodland walk through the Falls of Clyde Nature Reserve.

Difficult to detect when the trees are in leaf is Corra Castle. Corra Castle has been perched precariously 100 feet above the Corra Linn since the 15th century. The ruined castle is now home to Debenton bats. You shouldn't make any attempt to enter the castle.

In 1651 it was getting out of Corra Castle that was James Somerville's problem. James, on his way to fight for the beleaguered cause of Charles II, stopped off to bid farewell to his love Martha Bannatyne. When James tried to leave Martha refused to have the drawbridge lowered and James was trapped. Martha and James were later married. Looking at the castle it would appear that James didn't try too hard to escape Martha's clutches.

Unless it is one of those very occasional days, generally in August, when Corehouse is open to the public, you will have to be content with just a distant glimpse of the Edward Blore designed mansion house. Details of the dates of tours can be obtained from the Lanark Tourist Information Centre.

From this side of the river you have a close-up view of the Corra Linn. It was from here that William Wordsworth, his sister Dorothy and Samuel Coleridge experienced the awesome force. William composed a poem and Dorothy later wrote that she was struck with astonishment.

The next landmark downstream is the 17th century Clydesholm Bridge at Kirkfieldbank. A narrow hump backed bridge complete with pedestrian islands it was the only means of crossing the Clyde at this point until 1959.

Heading upstream again inevitably means a climb and it is steep to begin with but once Castlebank Park is reached it's all the way down again. Frustrating it might be but you'll be glad you're descending at this point and not coming up. There is a short climb into New Lanark however the views of the village and the river from the viewing platform overhanging the river make it worthwhile.

Bonnington Linn - the furthest upstream of the Falls of Clyde.

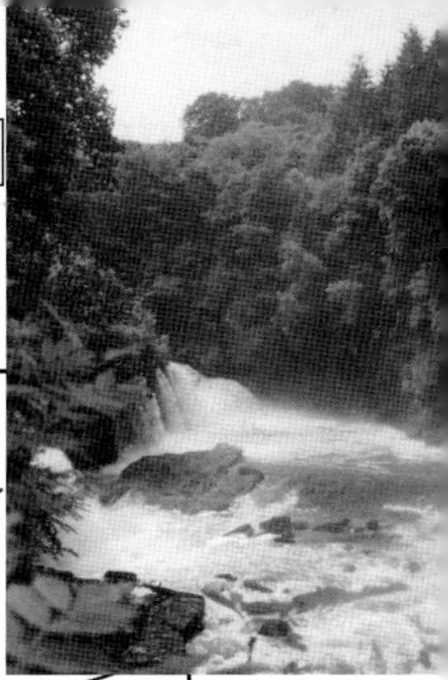

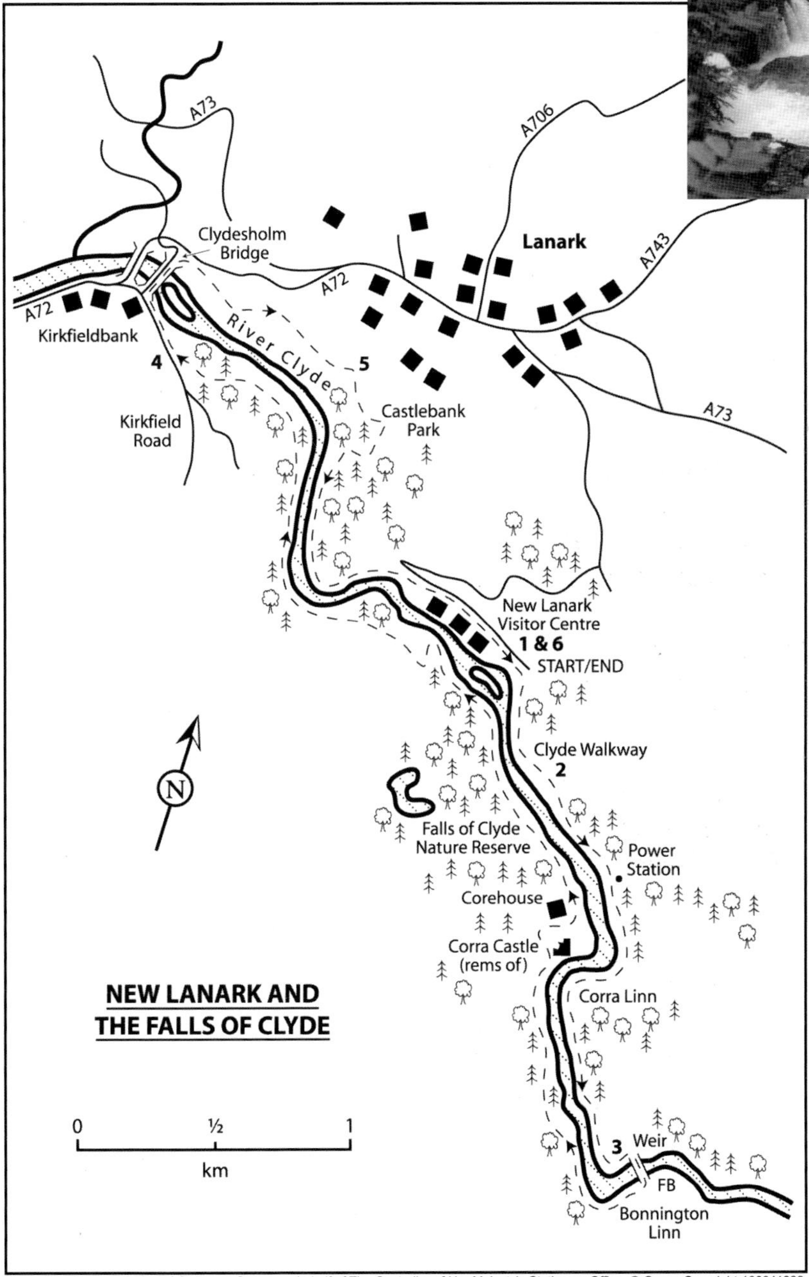

NEW LANARK AND THE FALLS OF CLYDE
A73
A706
A72
A743
A73
Clydesholm Bridge
Lanark
A72
Kirkfieldbank
River Clyde
4
5
Kirkfield Road
Castlebank Park
New Lanark Visitor Centre
1 & 6
START/END
Clyde Walkway
2
N
Falls of Clyde Nature Reserve
Power Station
Corehouse
Corra Castle (rems of)
Corra Linn
0
½
1
km
3
Weir
FB
Bonnington Linn

THE ROUTE

	Grid Ref.	Distance
1.	881 425	0

Start: New Lanark Visitor Centre.From visitor centre turn left down steps over canal and then left under walkway. Continue past water wheel and old schoolhouse. Ascend steps where canal enters hillside and follow river upstream.

2.   882 421   ⅓ mile

Just beyond boardwalk turn right and continue past power station and ascend steps to Corra Linn viewing area. Continue upstream to weir.

3.   884 406   1 ¾ miles

Cross weir and turn right downstream. Follow river downstream either on broad track or on gorge footpath (frequently closed). (In clearing for overhead cables footpath there is a path in a trench off to the left which leads to an estate road. Turn left. At entrance to reserve go to the right and eventually join minor road and continue straight on downhill into Kirkfieldbank). Otherwise continue straight on, going to the right for Corra Castle rather than going through gate. Follow path downstream. Eventually the path leaves the river bank and goes through woods. To get into Kirkfieldbank it is necessary to take up a faint track to the left and locate a hole in the wall. If you find yourself at a big locked gated you've missed it.

4.   869 436   5 ¾ miles

Proceed through Kirkfieldbank to river. Cross Clyde on old Clydesholm Bridge. Turn right through gate to take up the Clyde Walkway. Follow Walkway up hill past sewerage plant into Lanark. Footpath becomes narrow road. **NB** At the time of going to press access to this section is in dispute and you may be asked to follow an alternative.

5.   875 436   6 ¾ miles

After short distance on road take right into Castlebank Park. Follow road round to the left and just before the big house go to the right and follow path that twists downhill. Follow this path all the way to New Lanark.

6.   881 425   8 miles

End: New Lanark Visitor Centre.

THE THREE VALLEYS

Distance: 6 ½ miles.
Grade: moderate.
Starting/finishing Point: Lanark Interchange.
Maps: OS Landranger 72, OS Explorer 335. Compass not required.
Terrain: the route follows either quiet back roads or rights of way. The descent on the Stey Brae to the Mouse is steep as is the climb from the Mouse to Cartland. The rights of way can be muddy and are moderately inclined.

BY THE WAY

This is a very popular walk with local people. The route takes in the Mouse Valley, the Lee Valley and the Clyde Valley. It sweeps very steeply downhill out of Lanark on the Stey Brae into the picturesque Mouse Valley and just as steeply uphill out of it. On the way up you will notice poking out of the trees on the other side of the valley, Jerviswood House, built in 1593 it was the home of Covenanter Robert Baillie. Baillie was executed in 1684 for allegedly being one of the plotters of the Rye House Plot which sought to assassinate King Charles II in 1683. At the top of the brae a quiet road lined with beech trees offers good views and leads you to the hamlet of Cartland.

Next is the Lee Valley into which you descend on a right of way completely enclosed by high hedgerows and stands of birch. The Lee Valley has a broad flat floor and is dotted with large oaks so that it resembles parkland. The Lee Valley is very peaceful and feels separate from the world that surrounds it, which is just the way the owners of the nearby Lee Castle like it. The castle built for Sir Norman McDonald Lockhart of Lee in 1822 has the look of a schoolboy's toy castle.

The Lockhart family have had in their possession, since the 12th century, 'The Lee Penny'. The 'penny' is a stone that was part of a ransom demanded by Sir Symon Loccard from a Moorish prince for the return of his wife. The legend of the 'penny', which is supposed to have magical healing powers, was embellished by Sir Walter Scott in his novel *The Talisman*.

The inevitable climb out of the Lee Valley brings you onto a high spur of land that separates the Lee from the Clyde. There are good views of Lanark and you can follow the Clyde with your eye all the way out to the firth.

The Clyde Valley is surprisingly deep at this point and it is a long descent on back roads and a right of way known as The Ditches from the hamlet of Nemphlar to be by its banks at Kirkfieldbank. However it is the Mouse that you re-encounter first after a very steep final descent known as the Mouse Peth. The Mouse is bridged three times at this point. Telford's three arch

>>

THE ROUTE

	Grid Ref.	Distance
1.	886 436	0

Start: Lanark Railway Station. Turn left towards Lanark town centre and descend High Street. At point where High Street narrows turn right up Wide Close. Continue straight on to Greenside Street and then cross straight over Hope Street onto Waterloo Road and follow until it becomes the Stey Brae.

2.	881 446	¾ mile

Descend steeply on the Stey Brae to road. Turn right onto minor road. Follow road down to bridge and then fairly steeply uphill.

3.	877 456	1 ½ miles

At junction at the top of the hill turn left and follow road into Cartland. Turn left in Cartland and follow road to A73. Walk to the right for 20 yards or so and cross A73 to take up right of way.

4.	863 438	2 ½ miles

Follow right of way downhill. At the bottom of the hill continue straight on across the valley floor. Go through gate at cottage and ascend out of valley to road turn left and walk short distance to junction. Turn right and then left onto Hall Road. Take either the next left or the second left, just keep right at next junction past row of houses. Road becomes track at mobile phone mast. Follow track to road.

5.	867 444	4 ½ miles

Turn right onto road and descend steeply past Mousemill and caravan park.

6.	869 440	5 miles

Emerge at A72 in Kirkfieldbank. Cross A72 and go through gate to take up Clyde Walkway. **NB** At the time of going to press access to this section is in dispute and you may be asked to follow an alternative. Continue past sewerage plant and ascend fairly steeply into Lanark. Path becomes road follow road past Castelbank Park and follow round to the left beyond park into Lanark. Turn right onto High Street and follow to railway station.

7.	886 436	6 ½ miles

End: Railway Station.

>> Cartland Bridge towers above, there is the narrow road bridge on which you cross and there is the 'Roman bridge' that was actually built in 1649.

At Kirkfieldbank the route joins with the Clyde Valley Walkway which you follow uphill via Castlebank Park into Lanark.

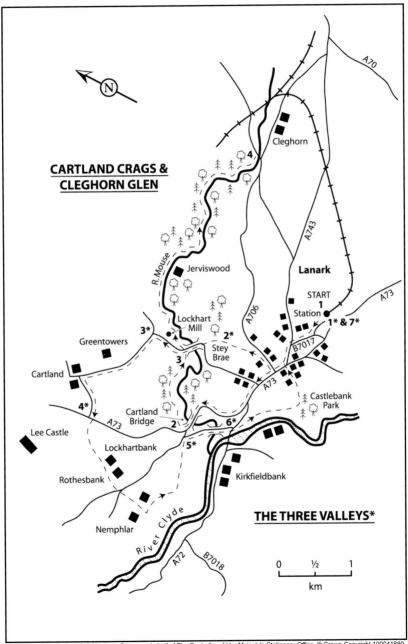

CARTLAND CRAGS & CLEGHORN GLEN

Cleghorn

Jerviswood

Lanark

START
1
Station

1* & 7*

R. Mouse

Greentowers

Lockhart Mill

3*

2*

Stey Brae

3

Cartland

Castlebank Park

4*

Cartland Bridge

2

6*

Lee Castle

Lockhartbank

5*

Rothesbank

Kirkfieldbank

Nemphlar

THE THREE VALLEYS*

River Clyde

0   ½   1
km

CARTLAND CRAGS AND CLEGHORN GLEN

Distance: 5 miles.

Grade: moderate.

Starting Point: Lanark Interchange or Cartland Bridge.

Finishing Point: A706, at Cleghorn.

Maps: OS Landranger 72, OS Explorer 335. Compass not required.

Terrain: footpaths are muddy in places and often blocked by fallen trees and swollen streams - extreme care must be taken. The first incline away from the Cartland Bridge is the only one.

Getting Back: from the Cleghorn end it is either a walk along the A706 into Lanark (2 miles - no pavement for the first ½ mile) or take the bus services 137 or 37 from the bus stop just over the bridge and round to the right; hourly service Mon-Sat, two hourly Sun.

BY THE WAY

If you start this walk in Lanark it will be with some relief that you'll reach Telford's Cartland Bridge and turn off the A73 and into the much more peaceful nature reserve. However as you do, take a look over the side of the bridge; the gorge is 125 feet deep. Legend has it that William Wallace hid in a cave in crags below but please do not make any attempt to find it. It is no surprise that the path takes a high line on the edge of this ancient woodland of oak, ash and hazel. This is one of the few places that you can see plants such as mountain mellick.

As the valley sides relax the path descends out of the wood into farmland and it is at this point that you can return to Lanark via Mousebank Road. This should be considered by those who do not have a head for heights or when the Mouse is in spate.

Beyond Mousebank Road the path skirts the side of the field nearest the river and is easily flooded. Once back in the woods you'll find plenty of evidence of how high the river can get as you clamber over a tangle of branches and fallen trees swept down river. After a period of heavy rain some of the small burns flowing into the Mouse can be very difficult to cross.

Unlike the first half of this walk the footpath remains very close to the river and it can feel quite intimidating above the waterfalls but this is nothing as compared with the 80 foot precipice that the path sits right on the edge of for a good few hundred yards in the section between Leechford Bridge (cross bridge if you wish to return to Lanark via Jerviswood) and Cleghorn Bridge. **It starts off easily enough but extreme care should be taken in this section, it is not suitable for children or for walking dogs.**

You will eventually emerge by the side of the A706 at the narrow Cleghorn Bridge built in 1661 and overlooking the picturesque Cleghorn Mill. From here it is either the bus or a walk along the A706 back into Lanark (2 miles).

THE ROUTE

        Grid Ref.   **Distance**
1. **886 436**   **0 miles**
Start: From railway station turn right towards Lanark Town Centre. Follow High Street downhill through narrow gap at St Nicholas Church and then follow the A73 downhill out of Lanark to Cartland Bridge.

2. **868 445**   **1 ½ miles**
On far side of Cartland Bridge cross road. Climb steep steps and then follow footpath on the edge of the woodland.

3. **877 450**   **2 ¼ miles**
Eventually the footpath emerges onto a minor road just uphill from a bridge. Descend towards bridge but do not cross the Mouse. (Cross the Mouse to follow road into Lanark). Cross stile into field. Stick with the Mouse following it upstream. Path re-enters woodland where path becomes indistinct and frequently blocked by fallen trees. Follow to metal bridge over Mouse.

4. **889 455**   **3 ½ miles**
Continue to follow river upstream or cross bridge to return to Lanark. As the path drifts away from the river it seems to split but stick with the edge of the woodland.

5. **899 458**   **4 ½ miles**
Follow footpath to the right over bridge/culvert when ahead is signposted as Private Garden. Then follow path round to right hugging stone wall. Footpath from now on is right on the edge of the gorge and is very exposed in places. The drop is considerable. Continue to A706 and cross Mouse on sandstone bridge. Round to the right is the bus stop for buses to Lanark.

6. **903 453**   **5 miles**
Finish: bus stop, Cleghorn.

THE DIFFERICK

Distance: 5 miles.
Grade: easy.
Starting/finishing Point: Greenrig Road.
Maps: OS Landranger 72, OS Explorer 335. Compass not required.
Terrain: the route follows a gently rising track (Roman road) and then quiet back roads.
Getting there: No public transport. Turn right onto Riverside Road at the far end of Kirkfieldbank just before bridge over Clyde (left just over the Clyde if coming from Lanark). Follow Riverside Road uphill out of Kirkfieldbank. Just beyond Newhouse Farm turn right and then after a short distance turn right again. Follow this road into dip and then to Greenrig at the top of the hill. Please park considerately.

BY THE WAY

The Differick is thought to be a short surviving section of a network of Roman roads that ultimately led to the large Castledykes fort near Ravenstruther. It is a credible claim for the road is characteristically straight and solid underfoot.

The Roman road rises to over 1000 feet just short of Boreland Hill which is obscured by forestry on your left. The whole of the lower Clyde Valley is on view and the hills of Argyll and the Trossachs are easily picked out. It was on Boreland Hill in March 1689 that the Cameronian and Covenanter Thomas Linning, who had just returned from exile in Holland, held an open air prayer meeting at which the Covenants were renewed.

The Differick ends at Low Boreland farm and the return follows pleasant tree lined back roads through farms. The views are now to the south to Tinto Hill and the Lowther Hills.

THE ROUTE

	Grid Ref.	Distance
1.	856 423	0 miles

Start: from Greenrig Road follow track between the houses. Follow track uphill and then down to Low Boreland farm. From farm follow road to crossroads.

2.	833 398	2 miles

At crossroads turn left and follow road all the way to Hawksland.

3. 849 399   3 ½ miles

At Hawksland turn left past row of houses known as Dickland. About 100 yards beyond houses 'Rebuilt by John Frater' take left fork and follow this road via Burnside Nursery to Greenrig.

4. 856 423   5 ½ miles

Finish: Greenrig.

see map p25

BLACKHILL

Distance: 3 miles.
Grade: moderate.
Starting/finishing Point: lay-by on minor road.
Maps: OS Landranger 72, OS Explorer 335. Compass not required.
Terrain: it is only moderately uphill for a short distance to the summit of Blackhill from where you continue over a grassy field and onto good surfaced lanes. Inclines are never more than moderate.

BY THE WAY

Blackhill might only be 290 metres high but it has been valued as a view point for over 4000 years. The view is remarkable in every direction and it is not difficult to appreciate the sense of security it must have offered the Iron Age people who built a fort on its summit.

On a clear frosty day the snow covered peaks of Arran appear particularly close in the west and the Cobbler, Ben Lomond and other northern hills can be very vivid.

Blackhill, the hill is topped by an Iron Age fort and may have been used along with Tinto to fix the date of the winter solstice.

It has been suggested that the Bronze Age people attached some spiritual significance to Blackhill and that is why they built a cairn on top of it to line up with the huge summit cairn on Tinto Hill in an attempt to fix the date of the winter solstice. A triangulation pillar now sits on top of the cairn.

After descending from the summit towards the transmitter it is onto peaceful hedgerow lined lanes that link farms, smallholdings and large private homes. Towards the end of the walk you may detect the remains of Stonebyres House, a once impressive 19th century mansion house. Although only occasionally occupied it was sold and demolished in 1935.

THE ROUTE

	Grid Ref.	Distance
1.	834 431	0

Start: lay-by, minor road. Cross stile and follow track up hill. Track becomes indistinct and rutted but just follow the rising ground to triangulation pillar.

2.	832 435	½ mile

From triangulation pillar proceed to high point to the north east. Descend by following the line of gorse but stay uphill of the gorse and aim as though you are going to pass the transmitter on the right.

3.	833 442	1 mile

In small group of trees in the corner of the field go round to the right to take up track lined by beeches. Follow downhill to gate. Continue through gate and follow narrow farm track straight-on to junction.

4.	837 439	1 ½ mile

At junction turn left and then left again and continue to descend. Road hooks round to the right and starts to ascend. At next junction turn right uphill. In trees not far beyond small park turn left over narrow bridge that has high fences for sides then follow track round field to road.

5.	843 437	2 miles

Turn right uphill and follow road to gates and B7018. Turn right onto B7018 and follow uphill. Leave B7018 for minor road which goes steeply uphill to return to lay-by.

6.	834 431	3 ½ miles

End: lay-by, minor road.

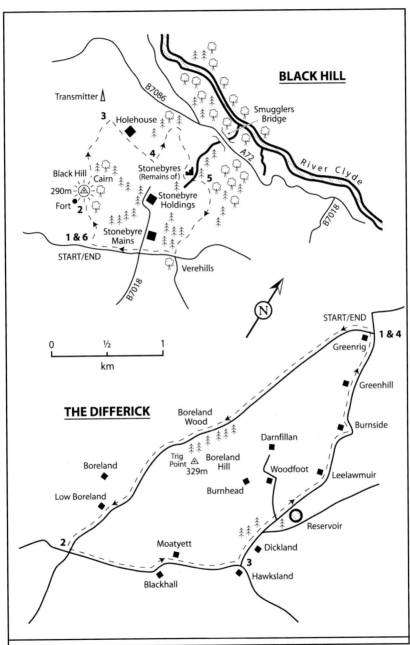

BLACK HILL

Transmitter Δ

3 Holehouse

4

Black Hill
Cairn
290m
Fort **2**

Stonebyres
(Remains of)

5

Stonebyre
Holdings

1 & 6 Stonebyre
Mains

START/END

Verehills

B7086

Smugglers
Bridge

A72

River Clyde

B7018

B7018

0   ½   1
km

N

THE DIFFERICK

Boreland
Wood

Boreland

Low Boreland

2

Trig
Point Δ
329m

Boreland
Hill

Burnhead

Moatyett

Blackhall

3

Darnfillan

Woodfoot

Hawksland

Dickland

Reservoir

Leelawmuir

Burnside

Greenhill

Greenrig

START/END
1 & 4

THE CLYDE WALKWAY - NEW LANARK/LANARK TO CROSSFORD

Distance: 5 miles.
Grade: easy.
Starting point: New Lanark Visitor Centre/Castlebank Park, Lanark.
Finishing point: Lanark Road, Crossford.
Maps: OS Landranger 72, OS Explorer 335. Compass not required.
Terrain: way-marked footpath - muddy in places.

BY THE WAY

It is hoped that at some point the Clyde Walkway will form a continuous walking route following the Clyde to link the Southern Upland Way to the West Highland Way. The idea of a Clyde Walkway was first mooted in the early seventies but it will not be long now until it is possible to walk from New Lanark to Glasgow as the last link is put in place just north of Crossford. Meanwhile the walkway can be enjoyed between New Lanark or Lanark and Crossford.

The highlight of the walk is the Stonebyre Falls the furthest downstream of the Falls of Clyde; some people reckon them to be the finest of the Falls of Clyde even though they have been much diminished by the Stonebyres Hydro-electric power station.

THE ROUTE

	Grid Ref.	Distance
1.	881 425	0

Start: New Lanark Visitor Centre. Walk uphill from the visitor centre to leave New Lanark via the road. Just before first bend turn left to join Clyde Walkway and follow all the way to Castlebank Park.

2.	875 434	1 ¼ mile

Turn left in Castlebank Park and then after a few hundred yards leave park and turn left downhill. Follow road to its conclusion and then take up footpath that continues downhill to emerge at Clydesholm Bridge. NB at time of going to press access to footpath between sewerage works and bridge is in dispute and you may be directed to follow an alternative.

3. 869 440   2 miles

Cross Clyde and follow road through Kirkfieldbank. After about ¾ mile go off to the right through the gate and follow the narrow access road to the weir. Cross Clyde once again and follow Clyde Walkway downstream to Crossford. Cross bridge for village.

4. 826 464   5 miles

End: Lanark Road, Crossford.

no map

Walking by the Clyde

THE CLYDE VALLEY
(WITH LISTINGS FOR CARLUKE AND BRAIDWOOD)
ROUTES

CROSSFORD

Crossford lies at the heart of what has come to be known as Orchard Country or the Garden Valley. Sheltered and deep in fertile alluvium this section of the Clyde Valley has been known for fruit growing since Roman times. Merlin sang about the orchards of the Clyde in the 6th century and the Venerable mentions them in a 8th century verse.

In the spring the display of blossom on the apple and cherry trees is still an impressive sight and in the late summer plums are sold from the roadside. There are opportunities to pick your own strawberries but today it is garden centres selling exotic plants and soup from their glasshouses, rather than tomatoes, that is the real commercial concern.

GETTING THERE
Road

From Glasgow: leave the M74 at junction 7 and follow the A72, Clyde Valley Tourist Route to Crossford.

From Edinburgh: leave the M8 at junction 6, Newhouse and follow A73 through Newmains and Carluke to Braidwood. Turn right in Braidwood at the Station Inn and follow the B7056 to Crossford.

Bus

HAD Coaches has an hourly service (Mon-Sat) from Lanark Interchange/Hamilton BS to Crossford. On Sundays it is reduced to a three hourly service.

For all public transport enquiries call Traveline 0870 608 2 608

EATING AND DRINKING
Crossford (01555 -)

Tillitudlem Inn, 14 Lanark Road, Crossford ~ 860555

Braidwood (01555 -)

Station Inn, 43 Lanark Road ~ 772105

Headspoint Nursery, Lanark Road ~ 772303

La Piazza Pizzeria, 33 Lanark Road ~ 750001

Scott's Country Style Restaurant, Lanark Road ~ 771292

Carluke (01555 -)
Platter Restaurant, 2 High St ~ 759900
Monsoon, 1-5 Carnwarth Road ~ 751715
Ming Hong Chinese Restaurant, 44 High St ~ 771042
The Chardonnay Restaurant, 17 Kirkton St ~ 751006

STAYING
Wallace Hotel, Yieldshields Road, Roadmeetings, Carluke ~ 01555 773000
The Tower of Halbar, Braidwood Road, Carluke ~ 0845 900 0194

FIDDLERS GILL
Distance: 7½ miles.
Grade: moderate.
Starting/finishing point: car park to the rear of the lawnmower/bicycle shop, Crossford.
Maps: OS Landranger 72, OS Explorer 343.
Terrain: good footpaths and quiet back roads.

BY THE WAY
This is a very pleasant walk combining a section of the Clyde Walkway, little used roads and peaceful wooded lanes of the eastern slopes of the Clyde Valley. The village of Braidwood is a good halfway point as the small loch just beyond the village centre is a great picnic spot or if you walk a little further, the Station Inn at the junction of the B7056 and A73,will provide a warmer lunch.

>> p31

Tower of Hallbar, a medieval tower house that has been sensitively converted to holiday accommodation.

THE ROUTE

	Grid Ref.	Distance
1.	826 467	0 miles

Start: car park to the rear of lawnmower/bicycle shop. Turn left out of car park and then turn left onto Lanark Road. Follow Lanark Road for 400 yards and turn left for Braidwood, B7056. Cross Clyde and continue for a further 300 yards.

| 2. | 831 466 | ⅔ mile |

Turn left down driveway signed as Holmlea and Ardfern. Follow driveway to white gate. At White Gate turn right over footbridge and then turn left onto gravel drive. Follow gravel drive to house and then follow footpath to the left of high hedge to be by the Clyde. Follow Clyde downstream. Eventually path climbs away from Clyde and crosses a field. Stick to right hand edge of field. Do not join tarmac driveway at the far end of the field but take up pronounced track to the left and follow to junction with minor road.

| 3. | 826 478 | 2 ½ miles |

Turn right onto minor road and follow to fork in the road. Take left fork and follow steeply uphill to T-junction. Turn right and follow for 500 yards to T-junction. Turn left and follow road over bridge into Braidwood. In Braidwood follow main street uphill to small wooded loch - good picnic site.

| 4. | 846 482 | 4 ½ miles |

To continue with walk turn right into Loch Avenue and follow road round to right and down past school. Just beyond school follow Fiddler's Gill right of way to the left. Follow to junction with another footpath in woodland high above the Fiddler's Gill. Turn right and follow footpath downstream. At bungalow follow right of way sign for St. Oswald's through gate to the left of bungalow. Footpath descends steeply and then descends through a field. Emerge onto minor road/drive turn left downhill and continue to footbridge over burn. Climb from footbridge to old road.

| 5. | 844 467 | 6 miles |

Turn right onto old road (closed to traffic) and follow through woodland past small holdings and farms to T-junction. Turn right and then at next T-junction turn left to retrace route into Crossford.

| 6. | 826 467 | 7 ½ miles |

End: car park, Crossford.

The return from Braidwood follows the Fiddler's Gill and this is where the walking is most pleasant especially since it is downhill most of the way. The woodlands that hang on the steep slopes by the Fiddler's Gill are valued as a habitat for rare beetles, the uncommon willow tit and green woodpecker.

St. Oswald's Chapel may sound intriguing but it is now no more than a conventional house. There is however a detour to Hallbar Tower, a medieval tower house refurbished as unique holiday accommodation; an information board explains all. At one point it would have been reasonable to return from Hallbar Tower along the B7056 but that road is much busier now and visibility is limited and therefore not recommended. It's best to retreat and continue with the route as described.

see map p33

JOCK'S GILL
Distance: 2 miles (3 miles including detour to General Roy Monument).
Grade: easy.
Starting/finishing point: Carluke railway station.
Maps: OS Landranger 72, OS Explorer 343.
Terrain: quiet back roads and woodland footpaths.

GETTING THERE:
Train
The walk starts from Carluke railway station and there are two trains an hour from Glasgow Central, Monday to Saturday and an hourly service on Sundays.
Road
From Carluke Cross go south on Kirkton Road (A73) and take next right, Station Road, and follow for about 600 yards.

BY THE WAY
It can be dank and damp in the woodland by Jock's Gill but that's the way plants such as golden saxifrage and horsetail like it. The walk passes through what is considered to be an excellent example of semi-natural deciduous woodland. The woodland is therefore a National Nature Reserve and under the protection of Scottish Natural Heritage.

Another point of interest away from the woodland (involves a detour) is Miltonhead the birthplace of Major-General William Roy, the man who is considered to be the father of the Ordnance Survey. As a young engineer in 1747 Roy was sent to map the Scottish Highlands to aid the army in its patrolling of the area in the aftermath of the 1745 Jacobite rebellion. A task that took him eight years. An Ordnance Survey triangulation pillar, which is more usually found on hill tops, marks the site of his family home.

THE ROUTE

	Grid Ref.	Distance
1.	840 502	0

Start: Carluke Railway Station.Leave railway station by turning left downhill under railway bridge.

	Grid Ref.	Distance
2.	837 500	300 yards

Just over stone bridge go to the right onto rough road. Follow to another smaller stone bridge but turn left through gate before crossing it. Follow the burn downstream through woodland past golf course. Footpath leaves burn just beyond metal footbridge. Follow footpath through gate and onto broader track to T-junction. (Turn right for detour to General Roy Monument).

	Grid Ref.	Distance
3.	829 497	1 mile

Turn left and follow road for about 750 yards, then turn left and follow this road all the way to railway station.

	Grid Ref.	Distance
4.	840 502	2 miles (3 miles including detour)

Finish: Carluke Railway Station.

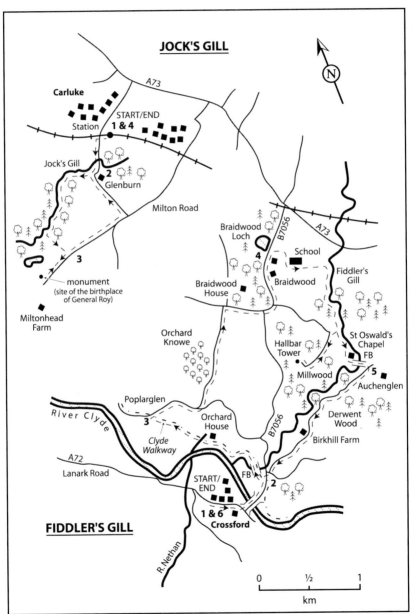

JOCK'S GILL

N

Carluke

A73

START/END
1 & 4

Station

Jock's Gill

2
Glenburn

Milton Road

3

monument
(site of the birthplace
of General Roy)

Miltonhead
Farm

Braidwood
Loch

B7056

A73

4

School

Braidwood

Fiddler's
Gill

Braidwood
House

Orchard
Knowe

Hallbar
Tower

St Oswald's
Chapel

FB

Millwood

5

Auchenglen

Poplarglen

River Clyde

3

Orchard
House

Clyde
Walkway

A72
Lanark Road

B7056

Derwent
Wood

Birkhill Farm

START/
END

FB

2

1 & 6
Crossford

FIDDLER'S GILL

R. Nethan

0   ½   1

km

CRAIGNETHAN CASTLE

Distance: 4 miles.

Grade: moderate.

Starting/finishing point: car park to the rear of the lawnmower/bicycle shop, Crossford.

Maps: OS Landranger 72, OS Explorer 343 (recommended). Alternative return requires OS Explorer 335. Compass not required.

Terrain: moderate climb to castle on narrow footpath. From then on walk follows the tarred castle drive, an old railway track bed and forestry tracks. Towards the end of the walk the tracks can be very muddy.

BY THE WAY

After a short walk through Crossford you cross the River Nethan just as it is about to join the River Clyde and then follow it up stream. The path climbs almost from the outset, to leave the river far below in a gorge that it has easily cut for itself from the surrounding carboniferous rock.

It is only in the winter that you are likely to be able to catch a glimpse of the river and the bottom of the gorge for in summer the gorge is obscured by a dense and impressive canopy of trees. The autumn display of colour is particularly impressive.

There is a rich ground flora dominated by bluebells and bright yellow broom but there are also the less commonplace wood fescue, bird's nest orchid and great horsetail to be sought out

At first sight across a kink in the gorge the castle seems to have been built in the perfect position surrounded on three sides by steep ravines but as you complete the final climb up to it, its major weakness is apparent - the ground on the remaining side is higher and from there, there is an excellent view of inside the curtain wall. The castle was therefore particularly vulnerable to attack by artillery.

With a collection of imposing towers, ruined ramparts and a deep ditch there is enough of Craignethan castle left to take up an hour of your time. A brief but excellent guidebook is available form the castle shop. Begun in 1530 by Sir James Hamiltlon of Finnart, it was the last private fortress to be built in Scotland.

A distinctive feature of its defences, and unique in Britain is the castle's *caponier*. Situated in the ditch that defends the weak west side, it was hoped that the ditch could be scoured by hand-gunners secure in this vaulted chamber.

The castle was captured and recaptured several times in a fifty-year period of military activity, but every time without a fight. The interest in the castle was due to the Hamiltons' support for Mary Queen of Scots after her abdication in 1567 and she is known to have been sheltered here in May 1568.

Craignethan Castle may or may not have provided Sir Walter Scott with the inspiration for 'Tillietudlem Castle' which features in his book *Old Mortality* but the link has grown so strong that the hamlet closest to the castle has adopted the name Tillietudlem and the castle is often referred to as Tillietudlem Castle. It was also rumoured that Sir Walter Scott contemplated the castle as a possible home but plumped for Abbotsford instead.

There is a choice for the return to Crossford. Either you can descend the steep braes into the Nethan Valley, a hidden pocket, where a hint of an older more sedate agrarian world still lingers. Or you can take the more pleasant and easier, if a little unremarkable, route along the track bed of an old branch line that ran from Ferniegair to Brocketsbrae, and then through commercial forestry to return to the Clyde Valley. There are good views of Tinto and the Clyde Valley from the high ground on both routes.

Craignethan
Castle

THE ROUTE

	Grid Ref.	Distance
1.	827 467	0

Start: car park to the rear of lawnmower/bicycle shop. From car park proceed to Lanark Road. Turn right and follow Lanark Road, north, out of Crossford.

| 2. | 824 470 | 400 yards |

Cross Lanark Road just beyond Tillietudlem Inn and then cross River Nethan.

| 3. | 824 471 | 450 yards |

Cross stile into Nethan Gorge Nature Reserve and follow footpath upstream. Footpath dips to cross the Craignethan Burn and then climbs to castle.

| 4. | 816 463 | 1 mile |

From castle climb steep red drive and follow red drive until it takes a sharp turn to the left. Alternative outlined below.

| 5. | 808 462 | 1 ½ miles |

Follow obvious track to gate. Go through gate and turn right onto old railway track bed. Follow track for about ½ mile.

| 6. | 803 470 | 2 miles |

Turn right off track bed into forestry plantation and follow broad forest track until it forks - not marked on map. Take left fork and follow track through and out of plantation.

| 7. | 816 471 | 3 miles |

In open country the track sinks into a hedge lined lane. Track can be very muddy. Track swings to right at barn. 200 yards beyond the barn turn right into unfenced field and follow left hand field margin south.

| 8. | 824 472 | 3 ¾ miles |

Descend steeply to gate. Go through gate and turn right onto the A72 (Lanark Road). For 100 yards or so there is no pavement, so take care. Retrace Lanark Road to car park.

| 9. | 827 467 | 4 miles |

End: Car park, Crossford.

ALTERNATIVE RETURN

From the castle follow the red drive all the way to the entrance/exit. Turn left and follow road downhill through the hamlet of Tillietudlem. Cross the River Nethan and then climb steeply to junction with Blair Road. Turn left and follow Blair Road downhill into Crosssford.

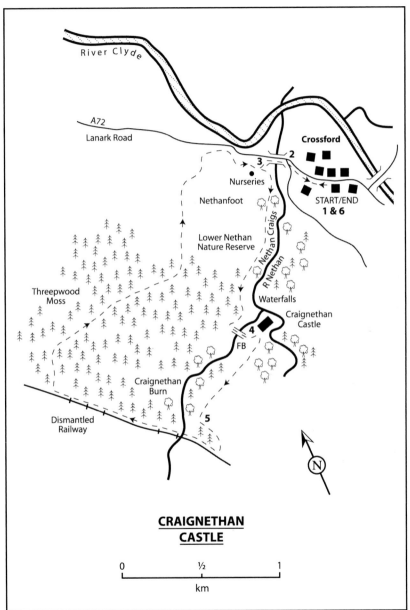

River Clyde

A72
Lanark Road

Crossford

3 **2**

Nurseries

Nethanfoot

**START/END
1 & 6**

Lower Nethan
Nature Reserve

Nethan Craigs

R Nethan

Threepwood
Moss

Waterfalls

Craignethan
Castle

4

FB

Craignethan
Burn

Dismantled
Railway

5

N

CRAIGNETHAN CASTLE

0   ½   1

km

THE TINTO

(WITH LISTINGS FOR THANKERTON, CARMICHAEL AND SYMINGTON)

ROUTES

TINTO HILL

On Tintock tap there is a mist
And in that mist there is a kist
And in that kist there is a cup
And in that cup there is a drap
Tak up the cup, drink aff the drap
And set the cup on Tintock tap. ANON

The summit cairn on Tinto Hill is the biggest in the country.

Tinto has a special place in the hearts of Lanarkshire people. Its graceful conical outline is easily picked out on the horizon to the south from throughout central Scotland. Not only is it a satisfying climb rewarded by exceptional views that stretch from Northern Ireland round to the Lake District and all the way north to Lochnagar but it is where local people come to mark the New Year, roll their Easter eggs and cure hangovers.

It seems Tinto has always been special. The Bronze Age people built Scotland's largest cairn on Tinto's summit; it is likely that they built it as a burial cairn but there have also been suggestions that it was used along with cairns on nearby hills to determine the exact day of the winter solstice.

Tinto Hill at 707 metres is the highest point entirely within Lanarkshire, Culter Fell a few miles to the south is higher but Culter has to be shared with Peebleshire and this has led to some local resentment of Culter Fell. An old couplet, "Twixt Tintock tap and Culter fell, there is just one third part of an ell" (Scot's Ell = 15") suggests that the heights of Culter Fell and Tinto are close and indeed an early survey of the hills seemed to confirm the truth of the rhyme, fixing the height of Tinto just above that of its rival. Unfortunately 70 years later a new survey established that Culter Fell was actually 135 feet higher. Ever since locals have encouraged the tradition of carrying a stone to Tinto's top to grow the hill to 2456 feet that is one foot higher than Culter Fell. At the present rate of growth it will take another 32 000 years.

Tinto might look higher simply because it is an isolated hill sitting apart from the jumble of peaks that make up the Southern Uplands. Unlike Culter Fell, Tinto sits to the north of the southern boundary fault and was formed by magma welling up from the earth's core to bulge under but not through the crust, a phenomenon known to geologists as a volcanic extrusion.

EATING AND DRINKING
(01899 - unless stated).
Tinto Hill Tearoom, Fallburn - at the foot of Tinto, by A73.
Carmichael Visitor Centre and Clan Farmhouse Kitchen, by A73 ~ 308336.

EATING, DRINKING AND STAYING
Tinto Hotel, Biggar Road Symington ~ 308454
Wyndales Hotel, by A72, by Symington ~ 308207
Cornhill House Hotel ~ 220001; Shieldhill Castle, Quothquan ~ 220035

STAYING
Carmichael Country Cottages, Carmichael ~ 308336
Crossridge Country Cottages, Carmichael ~ 01555 $^{880589}/_{880455}$

TINTO HILL FROM FALLBURN

Distance: 3 miles.

Grade: moderate/hard.

Starting point: car park Fallburn, 200 metres from A72.

Finishing point: summit of Tinto Hill.

Maps: OS Landranger 72, OS Explorer 335. Compass may be required.

Terrain: well worn and obvious route. Starts easily and then grows progressively steeper. Some sections are very loose underfoot.

Getting there: leave M74 at junction 7 and follow A72, Clyde Valley Tourist Route to Lanark. Leave M8 at junction 6 and follow A73 to Lanark. In Lanark follow signs for Biggar, A73. Cross Hyndford Bridge and turn left, after 4 miles turn right at Tinto Hill Tearoom. If you are coming from the south leave the M74 at junction 13, Abington. Follow signs for Lanark, A73 and after about 10 miles watch out for left turn at the Tinto Hill Tearoom.

Bus - Stuart's Coaches service No. 30 operates every ½ hours from Lanark Interchange to Thankerton.

BY THE WAY

This is by far the most popular route up Tinto Hill. The path is well worn and the underlying red felsite has been exposed meaning there is little doubt as to the way.

About half-a-mile in to the walk, look out for the iron-age fort on the left of the footpath. Its circular outline, however, of double ditches and ramparts is more obvious to the descending walker.

Just beyond the halfway point there is a choice. Either you can continue steeply up to the left or follow the path straight on round the magnificent sweep of Maurice's Cleuch, the steep scree slopes briefly give the feeling of being on a mountain rather than a hill especially in winter. It is not far before both routes join up again for the final pull to the summit. This route can be combined with the Lochlyvoch descent.

see map p43

TINTO HILL FROM WISTON

Distance: 2 miles, 450 metres of ascent.
Grade: hard.
Starting point: Wiston Lodge.
Finishing point:: summit of Tinto Hill.
Maps: OS Landranger 72, OS Explorer 335. Compass may be required.
Terrain: gentle at first through grassy fields turns steeply uphill, path very loose in places.
Getting there: Wiston is on the south side of Tinto. Coming from the north follow the directions for the Fallburn ascent and then the A73 for a further 5 miles before turning right when signed for Wiston. Coming from the south follow the A73 for about 5 miles before taking the left for Wiston.
Bus - a service (No. 30) operates every 1 ½ hours from Lanark Interchange to Wiston Road End. This service is operated by Stuart's coaches.

BY THE WAY

This route is as quiet as the Fallburn route is popular and it is hard to believe that it is the same hill. This route is much less obvious and the ascent is much steeper. In the upper reaches of the Pap Craig the path zigzags and is frequently obliterated by scree. Throughout the ascent there are fine views of the Clyde valley and the Southern Uplands.

see route & map p42-43

THE LOCHLYVOCH DESCENT

A pleasant alternative to descending the same way as you came up is to descend from the summit cairn west in the direction of the trig point. A fairly well defined grassy ridge makes navigation easy as you descend around the edge of the Martingill Cleuch. There is a slight rise over Lochlyvoch Hill and then from there it is steeply downhill for a short distance onto the track in the narrow pass known as the Howgate Mouth. Left for Wiston Lodge, then left at the road and finally take the left fork after 1 mile - 3 miles from summit to Wiston. Right for Fallburn and right at the road and follow road through Lochlyvoch Farm - 4 miles from summit to Fallburn.

THE ROUTE

	Grid Ref.	Distance
1.	956 322	0

Start: entrance to Wiston Lodge on Millrig Road. Go up drive towards Wiston Lodge and follow round to the left of lodge past wooden building known as Little Lodge and then follow signs for Tinto, Nature Trail, Caravan Park and Toilets. Continue straight on towards Tinto Hill.

2.	958 325	¼ mile

At junction of tracks at Scottish Water building continue straight on through gate. Stick to right hand margin of fields and continue in the direction of Tinto.

3.	957 329	½ mile

Once on open hillside follow obvious green swathe through heather towards rocky outcrop. Higher up the path becomes more indistinct as it zigzags up steep slope. Pick your way through loose gravel and scree and then follow double fence to summit. (The going is easier between fences).

4.	953 344	2 miles

End: summit of Tinto Hill.

Monument to the 3rd Lord Carmichael. *see p44*

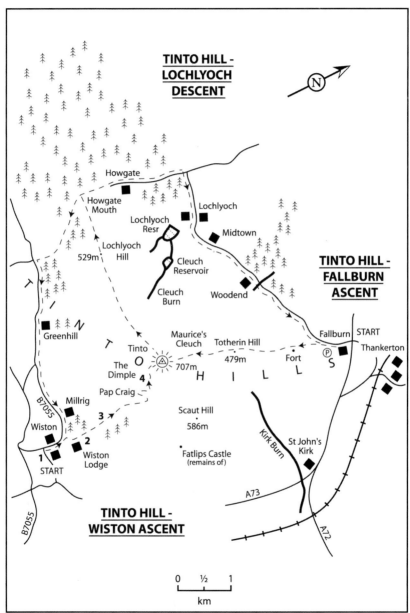

**TINTO HILL -
LOCHLYOCH
DESCENT**

N

Howgate

Howgate
Mouth

Lochlyoch

Lochlyoch
Resr

Midtown

Lochlyoch
529m Hill

Cleuch
Reservoir

Cleuch
Burn

Woodend

**TINTO HILL -
FALLBURN
ASCENT**

Greenhill

Maurice's
Cleuch

Totherin Hill

Fallburn START

Tinto

479m

Fort

P

Thankerton

The
Dimple **4**

707m

Pap Craig

Millrig

3

Scaut Hill

586m

Wiston

2

1

Wiston
Lodge

START

Fatlips Castle
(remains of)

Kirk Burn

St John's
Kirk

A73

**TINTO HILL -
WISTON ASCENT**

B7055

A72

0   ½   1

km

CARMICHAEL HISTORY WALK

Distance: 4 ½ miles.

Grade: easy/moderate.

Starting/finishing point: Carmichael Visitor Centre.

Maps: OS Explorer 335, OS Landranger 72 is of little help. Compass not required.

Terrain: level footpaths and estate roads to begin with. There is a moderate climb through woodland followed by a gentle rising walk across open hillside. Towards the end of the walk there is a very steep downhill.

Getting there: directions as for Tinto. Visitor Centre is 1 mile north of Tinto Hill Tearoom by the A73 - well signposted.

BY THE WAY

The start of this walk is easily picked out as much by the wind turbine by the A72 as the sign pointing out the Carmichael Visitor Centre and its Clan Farmhouse Kitchen. The visitor centre includes a souvenir shop and wax model exhibition detailing the Carmichael family history.

This has been the Carmichael family's patch since the 14th century. The nearby hamlet and the family take their name from a church dedicated to St Michael that was founded by Queen Margaret in 1058. The church was built on Kirk Hill which is on your right as you walk away from the visitor centre.

Not much further on, entirely enclosed by dense commercial forestry, is the Old Carmichael House which was built by the 3rd Earl of Hyndford in stages from 1734 - its predecessor was destroyed by Cromwell. The house is now ruined as the roof was removed in 1952 but there are plans to restore it and find a use for it.

At Westmains which is the present home of the chief of the clan Carmichael there is a very fine dovecot, built c. 1750, which stands 20 metres high and is reckoned to be one of the best examples in Scotland.

Also en route is the monument to the 2nd Earl of Hyndford on top of Carmichael Hill. The 2nd earl was a distinguished diplomat who was a Commissioner of the Treaty of Union of 1701 and was Ambassador to Russia and Vienna. He had a hand in making peace between Silesia and Prussia for which he was made a Knight of the Thistle by George II. The hill top also offers excellent views of the surrounding countryside and especially of Tinto.

There is ample parking at the Carmichael Visitor Centre so please only start the route from here. The route is signposted in places and marked by red and white tape, nevertheless the way ahead is unclear in places.

see map p46

THE ROUTE

	Grid Ref.	Distance
1.	948 388	0

Start: Carmichael Visitor Centre. Go round the end of the wax heritage museum and then go between the stables and the barn. Go round the rear of the barn onto a red gravel path. Turn right through gate and follow signs for Carmichael History Walk. Track snakes through woodland before turning steeply uphill towards red brick cottage. NB Tracks not marked on OS map.

2. 939 390 ¾ mile

Just before red brick cottage turn left towards trees.

3. 938 389 ¾ mile

At trees follow sign to the right and stick to the left of the old wall until you reach the drive. At drive turn left for ruins of Old Carmichael House.

4. 936 390 1 mile

Continue past the front of Carmichael House and follow signs around the edge of the building into trees. Go down couple of steps and then turn to the right and then to the left and cross small bridge (Note: Dogs graveyard). Follow widening drive through trees to another dirt track.

5. 933 388 1 ¼ miles

Turn right onto dirt track and then turn to the left onto main avenue at West Mains. Follow to Westgate.

6. 925 386 1 ¾ miles

At Westgate follow signs uphill in strip of broadleaved woodland more or less following the wall. The route is not especially clear at this point.

7. 923 392 2 ¼ miles

At the top of the climb follow sign to the right. Step over fence onto open hillside and follow rising ground to monument.

8. 933 395 3 miles

From monument make your way over to strip of commercial forestry. Go round the top of the strip and descend on the far side following the high deer fence steeply downhill.

9. 936 396 3 ¼ miles

At bottom of hill turn right onto estate track and continue between deer fences. Follow track round to the right and then down to the left past red brick cottage. Retrace outward route to visitor centre.

10. 948 388 4 ½ miles End: Carmichael Visitor Centre.

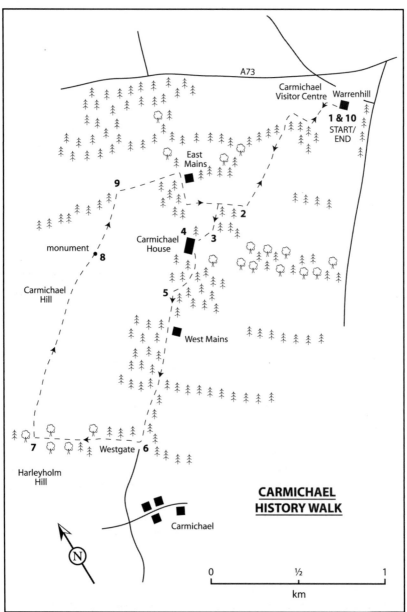

A73

Carmichael
Visitor Centre   Warrenhill

1 & 10
START/
END

East
Mains

9

2

4   3

monument

Carmichael
House

8

Carmichael
Hill

5

West Mains

7   Westgate   6

Harleyholm
Hill

**CARMICHAEL
HISTORY WALK**

Carmichael

N

0   ½   1

km

THE BIGGAR
(WITH LISTINGS FOR BROUGHTON AND SKIRLING)
ROUTES

BIGGAR

Biggar is an open and inviting town that nestles on a high plain between the Clyde and the Tweed. Its wide medieval High Street bristles with activity and curiosities. For a town made a burgh of barony in 1451 it seems peculiarly vulnerable to attack but perhaps congeniality was its defence. Several Scottish sovereigns are known to have enjoyed hunting in this area staying at the nearby Boghall Castle.

The feudal Lords of Biggar were the Flemings. The Flemings occupied Boghall Castle and were responsible for the building of the town's St Mary's Church in 1545, the last collegiate church to be built in Scotland. A Fleming daughter, Mary, was selected to accompany the young Mary Queen of Scots to France in 1548. At the annual Biggar Gala Day a local girl is crowned the Fleming Queen.

Biggar is a town that takes its heritage seriously. Five museums are to be found in the town and all but one are maintained and run by the voluntary Biggar Museum Trust, which is also responsible for Brownsbank Cottage, the last home of Hugh MacDairmaid at nearby Candy Mill and the John Buchan Centre in Broughton.

The Cadger's Brig.

BIGGAR'S MUSEUMS

Moat Park Heritage Centre:
a display of models that illustrate Clydesdale's geological formation and its Roman and Iron Age heritage. Housed in a former church it also contains the impressive Moffat Menzies tapestry.

Gladstone Court:
a hands-on museum that recreates the 19th century. A Victorian street with typical shops and a Victorian schoolroom are part of the experience.

The Albion Museum and Archive:
the Albion Motor Company was started with a bond on a local farm. The museum exploits this link and has a few vintage Albion vehicles on display. It also houses the Albion Archive - the complete records of the Albion Motor Company.

Greenhill Covenanters' House:
this 17th century house was built in its original location near Wiston on the south side of Tinto during the Killing Times, a bloody period when people who supported the National Covenant and its aim of defending the Presbyterian form of worship were hunted down by Government troops and often summarily executed. The museum tries to shed some light on this period and has a copy of the National Covenant signed in 1638.

Gasworks Museum (National Museums of Scotland)**:**
built in 1839 the Biggar gasworks are the only preserved gasworks in Scotland.

GETTING THERE

Road: From Edinburgh follow the A702 from the centre of Edinburgh for 29 miles. From Glasgow leave the M74 at junction 7, Larkhall and follow the A72 Clyde Valley Tourist Route to Lanark. From Lanark follow the A73 over the Hyndford Bridge, then take the left to rejoin the A72 after about 4 miles for Symington and Biggar. Follow all the way to A702 and then turn left for Biggar. From the south leave the M74 at junction 13, Abington and follow the A702(T) north for 12 miles to Biggar via Lamington and Coulter.

Bus - **McEwan's Coaches** operate 9 buses daily, Monday to Saturday and 4 on a Sunday from Edinburgh (Waterloo Place) to Biggar (Corn Exchange).
Irvine's Coaches and **HAD Coaches** between them operate an hourly service, Monday to Saturday, from Lanark Interchange to Biggar, Corn Exchange.

EATING AND DRINKING

Biggar (01899 -)
G&M Fast Foods, 124 High St ~ 220133
Golden Fry Chip Shop, 110 High St ~ 220996
La Campannina, 55 High St ~ 221032
Taj Mahal, 101 High St ~ 220801
The Oriental, 3 Park Place ~ 221894

The Crown, 109 High St ~ 220116
Cross Keys, 1 High St ~ 220176
Townhead Café, 152 High St ~ 220159
The Coffee Spot, 152 High St ~ 221902
Teas and snacks are also served in the Gillespie Centre, High St.

Broughton (01899 -)
Laurel Bank Tearoom, Main Street ~ 830462

EATING, DRINKING AND STAYING
Biggar (01899 -)
Elphinstone Hotel, 145 High Street ~ 220044
Shieldhill House, Quothquan ~ 220035
Cornhill House, Coulter ~ 220001
Clydesdale Hotel, 76 High St ~ 221100

Skirling(01899 -)
Skirling House ~ 860274

STAYING
Biggar (01899 -)
Daleside B&B, 165 High Street ~ 220097
Cormiston Farm Cottage B&B, Cormiston Road ~ 220200
Lindsaylands House B&B ~ 220033
Glen Avon B&B, 2A Boghall Ave ~ 220954
Larchfield, Hartree Road ~ 220726

HILLRIDGE, LANGLEES AND CORMISTON

Distance: 5 miles.

Grade: easy.

Starting point/finishing point: Corn Exchange, High Street, Biggar.

Maps: OS Explorer 336, OS Landranger 72. Compass not required.

Terrain: farm tracks and gentle walking at the margins of grassy fields. Return is along quiet roads.

BY THE WAY

This is a delightful walk that lets you really enjoy the beautiful landscape that surrounds Biggar. Either Tinto Hill or Culter Fell is visible for much of the walk but otherwise there is not much to watch out for and the walk through green fields and along tracks lined by beech trees can be enjoyed for its own sake.

At the point where you turn off Cormiston Road left onto Lindsaylands Road continue straight on for 200 yards or so to Culter Motte Hill. The motte, maintained by Historic Scotland, seems at first to be in the wrong place for a defensive site but once on top you can appreciate the excellent view its occupants would have had up and down the Clyde and through to the Tweed. One of its original occupants may have been Alexander de Cutir an Anglo-Norman lord granted lands by David I in the 12th century. Also be sure to cross the 16th century Cadgers Brig on your return to Biggar.

THE ROUTE

	Grid Ref.	Distance
1.	043 378	0

Start: Biggar Corn Exchange Cross High Street and turn left and then follow Kirkstyle round to the right. Cross road to heritage centre and then descend onto Burn Braes. Cross stream and follow road that goes to left of car park at Greenhill Covenanters Museum signed as BCPN - Hillridge 1 km, Huntfield 3.5km. Follow road all the way to Hillridge Farm.

	Grid Ref.	Distance
2.	029 389	1 mile

Continue past Hillridge Farm and follow the signs straight on for BCPN - Springfield 600 m, Biggar 2.5 km. Track continues until you encounter a fourth gate . Go through awkward fourth gate and step over burn. Follow ditch across field to line of beeches ahead. Turn left onto track signed for Springfield 200 m, Biggar 2 km.

3.   024 383   1 ¾ miles

Continue straight on at Springfield Farm and follow farm track to gatehouse. Turn right at gatehouse onto tarmac drive. After a short distance turn right signed for Cormiston (Quothquan Road) 2 km .

4.   030 378   2 miles

Follow road uphill past Langlees Farm. Continue past Langlees Farm and continue straight on through gate at cottage. Follow tree lined lane uphill and then into field; stick with the left hand side of field.

5.   018 377   2 ½ miles

At bottom of field go through gates and then go gently uphill following fence to top end of this field. Go through gate to left and join track. Follow track through sheepfold and then follow left to road.

6.   011 374   3 miles

Turn left onto road signed Biggar 3.5 km, and follow downhill to junction with Lindsaylands Road. Turn left (Culter Motte Hill is a short detour straight-on) onto Lindsaylands Road and follow into Biggar.

7.   043 378   5 miles

End: Corn Exchange, Biggar.

see map p53

BIGGAR TO SHIELDHILL

Distance: 3 miles.

Grade: moderate.

Starting point: Corn Exchange, High Street, Biggar.

Finishing point: Shieldhill Road

Maps: OS Explorer 336, OS Landranger 72. Compass not required.

Terrain: farm tracks and indistinct footpath uphill through grassy fields; can be muddy at times. On the far side the track is obvious through heathery moor and woodland.

BY THE WAY

This route follows the Hillridge, Langless and Cormiston route as far as Hillridge Farm, from where it heads up hill to the low point between Temple Hill and Huntfield Hill. At the top there is a fine view of Biggar, the Broughton Heights and Culter Fell. To your left is the distinctive outline of Bizzyberry Hill a small rocky looking hill that was judged by Iron Age man to be the perfect place to build a fort.

The walk descends on far side through deep heather and between the stunted remains of trees that were blown down in the same storm that destroyed the Tay Bridge in 1839. The descent continues through woodland and on the tarmac drive past the impressive Huntfiled House to emerge onto Shieldhill Road.

THE ROUTE

	Grid Ref.	Distance
1.	043 378	0

Start: Biggar Corn Exchange. Cross High Street and turn left and then follow Kirkstyle round to the right. Cross road to heritage centre and then descend onto Burn Braes. Cross stream and follow road that goes to left of car park at Greenhill Covenanter's Museum signed as BCPN - Hillridge 1 km, Huntfield 3.5km. Follow road all the way to Hillridge Farm.

2.	027 389	1 mile

200 yards beyond Hillridge Farm turn right into field following the sign BCPN - Huntfield/Shieldhill 2 km. Stick with left hand side of the field as you climb. Cross stile at top end of field and then step over gate to your left and continue to brow of hill and then go through gate in the dyke. Search for rickety stile on other side of field and cross to join obvious track in the heather.

3.	020 396	1 ¾ miles

Follow obvious track downhill and then round to the left under a leaning beech tree. Continue to the edge of the woodland and go through black gate into woodland. Follow obvious track through woodland to white gates.

4.	014 401	2 ¼ miles

Go through first white gate and then continue straight-on and through second white gate. Follow tarmac drive downhill with Huntfield on your left and the Home Farm on your right to gatehouse.

5.	013 404	2 ½ miles

End: Shieldhill Road..

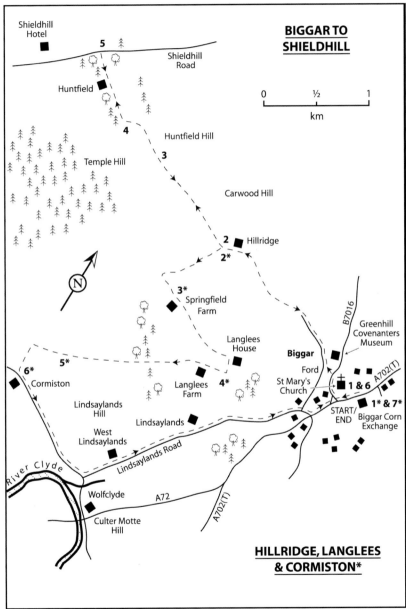

BIGGAR TO SHIELDHILL

0   ½   1
km

HILLRIDGE, LANGLEES & CORMISTON*

BIGGAR TO BROUGHTON

Distance: 5 miles.
Grade: easy.
Starting point: Corn Exchange, High Street, Biggar.
Finishing point: Main Street, Broughton.
Maps: OS Landranger 72, OS Explorer 336. Compass not required.
Terrain: level walk on a good surface.

BY THE WAY

A ride on the train from Biggar to Broughton is a treat that is never likely to be possible again but the consolation is that the track bed is still intact offering a very pleasant walk from Biggar to Broughton.

Apart from the gates there is no climbing on the former Biggar to Broughton railway line.

John Buchan who wrote among other things *The 39 Steps* holidayed with his family in Broughton and all around you is the scenery that may have inspired him to write his tales of adventure and pursuit. Ahead are the sweeping ridges and corries of the compact but steep Broughton Heights, to the south-east is bulky Broad Law and to the south is Culter Fell's mountain like satellite Cardon Hill.

You emerge in Broughton at the south end of the village. Further south in an old church is a museum also managed by the Biggar Museum Trust which is largely devoted to the Buchan family who still keep a holiday home in the village. The village's pretty centre is to the north where there is the general store and the Laurel Bank Tearoom.

You can walk back the way you came or you can phone a taxi (Lyne Taxis ~ 07771 756471 or Gracie Taxis ~ 01899 810207) or take the bus back to Biggar.

THE ROUTE

	Grid Ref.	Distance
1.	043 378	0

Start: Corn Exchange, Biggar. Follow St John's Loan, the road immediately to the right of the Corn Exchange as you look at it, past the school and into the park.

2.   045 374   ¼ mile

Follow tree lined footpath through golf course watching for a right turn about 100 yards short of the boating pond. Take this right and follow to the railway track just beyond the kiddies play area.

3.   048 370   ½ mile

Follow track bed east signed BCPN - Broughton 8 km. At the Broughton end go to the left in the coal yard and follow lane out to Main Street. NB at time of going to press the route through the coal yard is in dispute and an alternative may be provided.

4.   113 361   5 miles

End: Main Street, Broughton.

see map p59

SKIRLING TO BROUGHTON

Distance: 3 miles.
Grade: easy/moderate.
Starting point: Skirling Village Green.
Finishing point: Broughton Main Street.
Maps: OS Explorer 336, OS Landranger 72. Compass not required.
Terrain: footpath through grassy meadows and light woodland, indistinct in places.

BY THE WAY

With its village green Skirling has the definite feel of England rather than the Scottish Borders. Nevertheless the village green is a very appealing innovation that should have been replicated throughout Scotland.

The green is shaded by huge broad-leaved trees and on three sides the green is lined by low cottages. On the fourth side are the road and the village Kirk. Contributing further to the impression of a country idyll is the half timber, half stone Skirling House. Skirling House was built in 1908 for Lord Carmichael and designed by an Arts and Crafts architect. It incorporates such features as brass lamps and a village pump.

Skirling village green

Equally idyllic but in a more Scottish way is Broughton. With the hills bearing down on it the houses huddle together along the Main Street rather than relax around a village green.

This walk follows an old drove road that would have been used by farmers to drive their livestock to market in Edinburgh or Lanark or maybe even to one of Skirling's three annual agricultural fairs. Skirling at that time had two inns and many shops that would have been very tempting to drovers but Broughton would've been just as appealing. Perhaps they contrived a short days droving in order to stop in them both.

The drove road is a good place from which to appreciate the easy beauty of the Border hills and Broughton's favourable position among them. Indeed Broughton seems to have been favoured since at least the seventh century when St Llolann or St Maurice founded a church here. A vaulted chamber attached to the remnants of Broughton's ancient church has been rather optimistically declared as St Llolan's cell. The church is towards the end of the walk but you'll have to walk into the village to get the key for the cell from the village shop.

It has even been claimed that Broughton has associations with King Arthur and Merlin. Closer inspection of the OS map will reveal such place names as Merlindale the reputed resting place of the poet/magician Merlin (grave marked by a tree) and Altarstone the spot where St Kentigern is supposed to have baptised Merlin. To celebrate the link, Broughton's own brewery brews a Merlin's Ale but there is no longer a village pub in which to sample it.

THE ROUTE

	Grid Ref.	Distance
1.	076 390	0

Start: Skirling Village Green.Leave the village green from its north-east corner, i.e. top right with your back to Skirling House. Follow rough road round to the right and then uphill. Continue past Whinnybrae. Drover's road then winds its way through immature pines. Eventually you emerge from the trees to descend and cross the Kirklawhill Burn.

2. 088 382   1 mile

From the Kirklawhill Burn the drove road isn't apparent. Stick to left hand side of field and then follow ditch through middle of next field until drove road reappears. Aim to scuff top of narrow shelter belt of trees that comes up from Burnetland Farm.

3. 103 372   2 ¼ miles

The road is then obscured by gorse. Find a way to follow the strip of gorse up and over the shallow pass. On the other side descend through light woodland/meadow to old churchyard. Either go round or through churchyard and follow lane downhill to junction with B7016. From there it is a short distance to Broughton's Main Street.

4. 113 367   3 miles

End: Main Street, Broughton.

see map p59

BROUGHTON HEIGHTS

Distance: 6 ½ miles.

Grade: hard.

Starting/finishing point: car park at Shepherd's Cottage.

Maps: OS Explorer 336, OS Landranger 72. Compass required.

Terrain: footpaths and open hillside, steep at times.

BY THE WAY

The Broughton Heights rise so quickly that they seem taller than they actually are. In fact the highest point Pyked Stane Hill is only a mere 547 metres which is probably the main reason why they are delightfully overlooked.

A compact group of three hills and many more peaks the Broughton Heights form their own little world and when you are on the inside there is nothing else to see. On the undulating summit ridges the views are exceptional in all directions and are not often obscured by mist.

Walking in the Broughton Heights

Taking in all of the summits is not easy and a long detour is required from the main group to take in Pyked Stane Hill away to the north but the main group of Clover Law, Broomy Side, Hammer Head and Trahenna are linked by a well defined ridge and offer a very worthwhile day out.

There are many footpaths that cross the Heights and the most satisfying is the right of way over to Stobo from where you can return to Broughton by following the very quiet road via Dreva. From the road there is easy access to a prominent and still obvious Iron Age fort on Dreva Craig.

The best place to start a round of the Heights is from the car park just beyond Broughton Place. Brougton Place is a fine example of a Scottish Baronial tower house and a small part of it is open to the public as an art gallery. To reach the car park turn right off the A701 about 100 yards north of the Broughton Village Hall and follow the tarmac drive uphill through Broughton Place Farm. Beyond Broughton Place the road becomes a rough track but it only a short distance to the car park by Shepherds Cottage.

THE ROUTE

	Grid Ref.	Distance
1.	119 375	0

Start: Shepherd's Cottage - car park.Follow the obvious track away from the car park towards the small stand of pine trees. When the path dips leave the path and climb the slopes of Clover Law to your left. The easiest ground is to the right of the trees that go uphill from the Duck Pond. On attaining the ridge follow the fence up hill over the summit of Clover Law then down the other side to Cowiemuir Hass.

2.	124 394	1 ¼ miles

Cross fence and follow the grassy track bending away to the left. Join broad ridge and follow north over Broomy Side and Green Law to Pyked Stane Hill (trig point).

3.	124 411	2 ½ miles

From Pyked Stane Hill return to the Cowiemuir Hass by outward route.

4.	124 394	3 ¾ miles

A little below the Cowiemuir Hass on the south side is a John Buchan Way marker. Join broad path at marker and follow east to gate.

5.	127 393	4 miles

Turn right uphill at gate following the fence on to the shoulder of Hammer Head. Follow the fence over the summit of Hammer Head and round the broad undulating ridge over Green Lairs, Grey Yade and Trahenna Hill. Follow any one of a number of breaks in the heather downhill towards Shepherd's Cottage.

6.	119 375	6 ½ miles

End: Shepherd's Cottage.

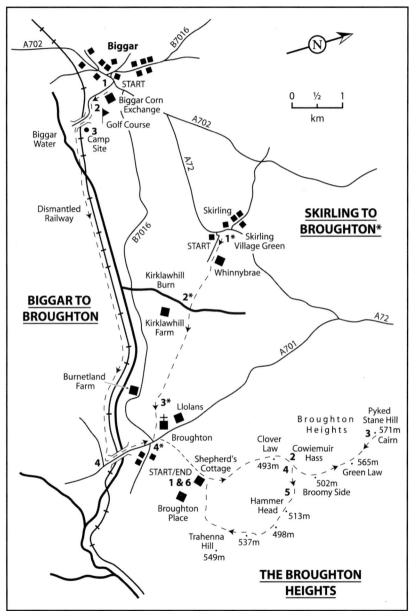

A702

Biggar

B7016

START
Biggar Corn
Exchange
Golf Course

A702

A72

Biggar
Water

Camp
Site

1

2

3

Dismantled
Railway

Skirling

**SKIRLING TO
BROUGHTON***

B7016

START

1*

Skirling
Village Green

Whinnybrae

Kirklawhill
Burn

2*

**BIGGAR TO
BROUGHTON**

Kirklawhill
Farm

A72

A701

Burnetland
Farm

3*

Llolans

Pyked
Stane Hill
571m
Cairn

Broughton
Heights

3

Broughton

4*

Clover
Law

Cowiemuir
Hass

565m
Green Law

4

Shepherd's
Cottage

493m

2

4

START/END

1 & 6

502m
Broomy Side

5

Broughton
Place

Hammer
Head

513m

Trahenna
Hill
549m

537m

498m

**THE BROUGHTON
HEIGHTS**

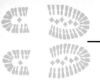

THE CULTER FELL
ROUTES

CULTER FELL
Culter Fell (748 metres), is a large sprawling and complex massif that sits astride the Clyde/Tweed watershed and the Peebleshire/Lanarkshire boundary. In Peebleshire it is largely ignored because it is lower than the likes of Broad Law and Dollar Law and conversely in Lanarkshire it is resented because it is higher than Tinto Hill. Culter Fell, however has many hidden corners that are a joy to explore and even if it were as popular an ascent as Tinto it would still be easy to find solitude in any one of its glens or on the ascent of one of the many ridges and satellite peaks.

Coulter village, at the foot of the Fell is a pleasant little village strung along the A702 with a surprising number of mansion houses in and around it. The church, which is about 300 yards beyond the village hall and on the right as you come to the end of the Cow Castle route, has a round churchyard which suggests that it predates the church by a considerable margin. Anthony Murray a prominent Covenanter is buried there as is the Victorian kleptomaniac Adam Sim. Sim built-up a large collection of all things antiquarian, by, some would suggest, doubtful means. Most were donated to the National Museum of Scotland but some still litter the grounds of his Coulter home.

GETTING THERE
Road - Coulter Village lies two miles south of Biggar on the A702(T); see directions for Biggar. See also individual routes for more detailed directions.
Public transport is not helpful for any of these walks.

EATING AND DRINKING
Coulter - see also Biggar (01899 -)
Culter Mill Restaurant ~ 220950
Murray's Dumpling Pot Tearoom,
Culter Park Farm ~ 221363

EATING AND STAYING
Cornhill House Hotel, Cornhill Road ~ 220001

Coulter Kirk

CULTER FELL FROM CULTER ALLERS
Distance: 7 ½ miles.
Grade: hard.
Starting point/finishing point: Culter Allers Farm.
Maps: OS Landranger Sheet 72, OS Explorer Sheet 336
Terrain: good track to begin with but mainly open hillside which can be boggy at times.

BY THE WAY
This is the standard way up and down Culter Fell and there is even a small lay-by for car parking; please don't take your car beyond this point.

For most of the way up you climb on a gently rising track which winds through woodland before emerging out onto open hillside where, in late summer, the heather is often deep and vibrant. From the first switchback there is a good view of the earth ramparts and mounds of an Iron Age fort. From the second switchback the view is even better as you look down on it.

Crossing the Glenharvie Moss may require a compass but the edge of the deep cleuch to your right is a good handrail and a good way of avoiding the tedious peat hags that cover the Moss.

THE ROUTE

	Grid Ref.	Distance
1.	031 311	0

Start: lay-by, Birthwood.Walk back along the road towards Culter Allers Farm.

| 2. | 032 310 | 250 yards |

Turn right towards farm and then follow right fork (tarmac). Go to the left at barns and through two gates. Second gate immediately to the right.

| 3. | 033 313 | 350 yards |

Once through gate good track zig-zags uphill and through woodland at first. Track straightens out to cross broad shoulder. Path climbs gently but there is a steep section to overcome the Tippet Knowe. Track is less obvious from here on but it more or less follows the fence. It is best though to drift to the right using the edge of the cleuch on the right as a handrail (avoids peat hags). On final steep ascent drift back towards fence to arrive at trig point.

| 4. | 053 291 | 3 miles |

Summit: Culter Fell **A.** From summit follow a bearing of 236° to join up with obvious track that services grouse shooting butts. Follow track downhill to dam. Turn right and follow reservoir road to Birthwood.OR **B.** Follow fence downhill to the south and over Moss Law to the Holm Nick (narrow pass) join path on west side and follow downhill. Follow track along the side of the reservoir and then follow reservoir road to Birthwood. OR **C.** In clear weather it is easy to follow the broad grassy ridge between the two options above which is actually the more natural option - the going is however hummocky and tussocky. Follow track by reservoir and then the road back to Birthwood.

| 5. | 031 310 | A. 7 miles B. 8 ½ miles C. 7 ½ miles |

End: Birthwood.

see map p65

Looking over the Culter Hills and the Culter Reservoir with Green Lowther in the distance.

CULTER FELL VIA CARDON HILL

Distance: 4 ½ miles.
Grade: hard.
Starting point: minor road close to entrance to Kilbucho House.
Finishing point: summit, Culter Fell.
Maps: OS Explorer 336, OS Landranger 72. Compass required.
Terrain: a good track gives way to steep open hillside. On the way between Cardon Hill and Culter Fell peat hags have to be negotiated and the ground can be boggy.

BY THE WAY

This is easily the hardest way up Culter Fell and consequently probably the least used. The reward for the extra effort is extensive views most of the way up as you follow a broad grassy ridge over the top of several bumps and Common Law. On two of the lumps there is visible evidence of an earthwork and an Iron Age fort.

The final climb to the summit of Cardon Hill is as steep a climb as you will encounter in the Southern Uplands. Indeed Cardon Hill may be far enough for some people as it is a long walk over Kings Bank Head and the Glenharvie Moss to the summit of Culter Fell and there is much boggy ground and peat hags to be negotiated. Those of you who are collecting Donalds will want to detour east, from the col between Cardon Hill and Culter Fell, to Chapelgill Fell.

Cardon Hill from Broughton

THE ROUTE

	Grid Ref.	Distance
1.	086 349	0

Start: minor road, 100 yards to the east of the entrance to Kilbucho House - not to be confused with Kilbucho Place. Go through gate and follow good track to the left of Trebetha Hill which becomes a wide grey forestry road. Follow forestry road to entrance of forestry.

	Grid Ref.	Distance
2.	085 335	1 mile

Turn uphill at entrance to forestry. At top end of forestry step over fence and proceed to the top of little knoll - Knowe Kniffling. Follow fence downhill keeping the trees on your left and then uphill to the top of Common Law.

	Grid Ref.	Distance
3.	080 324	1 ¾ miles

Sticking to the broad ridge (fence on left) descend once again and then climb very steeply uphill to the summit of Cardon Hill.

	Grid Ref.	Distance
4.	065 315	2 ¾ miles

From Cardon Hilll follow the fence south west to Birnies Bowrock (junction of fences). Continue south west following the fence over the Glenharvie Moss (peat hags). Follow the fence all the way to the summit of Culter Fell (trig point).

	Grid Ref.	Distance
5.	053 291	4 ½ miles

End: summit of Culter Fell.

Culter Waterhead

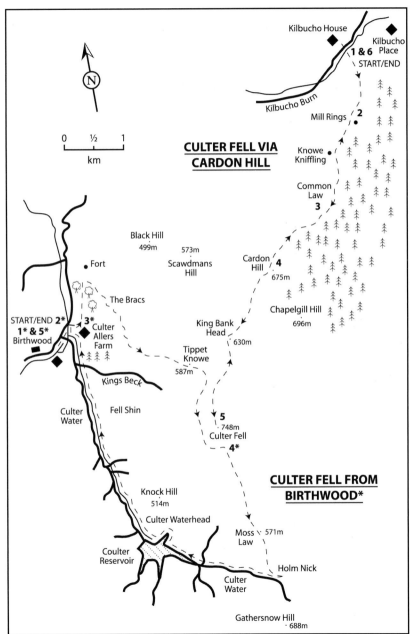

CULTER FELL VIA
CARDON HILL

CULTER FELL FROM
BIRTHWOOD*

0   ½   1
km

Kilbucho House
Kilbucho Place
1 & 6
START/END

Kilbucho Burn

Mill Rings   2

Knowe
Kniffling

Common
Law
3

Black Hill
499m   573m

Fort   Scawdmans
Hill

Cardon
Hill   4
675m

The Bracs

Chapelgill Hill
696m

START/END 2*
1* & 5*
Birthwood

3*
Culter
Allers
Farm

King Bank
Head
630m

Tippet
Knowe
587m

Kings Beck

Culter
Water

Fell Shin

5
· 748m
Culter Fell
4*

Knock Hill
· 514m

Culter Waterhead

Coulter
Reservoir

Moss \· 571m
Law

Holm Nick

Culter
Water

Gathersnow Hill
· 688m

COW CASTLE AND MITCHELL HILL

Distance: 6 miles.

Grade: easy/moderate.

Starting point/finishing point: Coulter Village Hall.

Maps: OS Landranger 72, OS Explorer 336. Compass not required.

Terrain: good tracks and quiet minor roads throughout.

BY THE WAY

This route leaves Coulter village for Nisbet and Snaip and then settles into a subtle crease between tiny but steep-sided foothills and Culter Fell. It was on these hillocks that Iron Age man built many forts and there are so many that the area could almost be described as an Iron Age metropolis. One such fort is Cow Castle which sits on top of the very first hillock on your left. It is a short stiff pull to the castle up a slope that was modified by Iron Age man to thwart attacks by warriors on horseback - basically they increased the gradient in places to interfere with a horse's stride.

The ancient and enigmatic Kilbucho Church lies not too far off the route. Now it is barely even a ruin and would seem to have had a fairly unremarkable existence except that its secluded location was favoured by outed Covenanter ministers.

THE ROUTE

	Grid Ref.	Distance
1.	025 338	0

Start: Coulter Village Hall. Turn left out of car park and then left again for Birthwood. Follow road to fork. Take left fork. Follow road to Nisbet Farm.

	Grid Ref.	Distance
2.	036 329	1 mile

Proceed through farmyard to left between house and barn and round the end of the barn to the right and leave farm through gate. Follow track off to the left and then after a short distance off to the right into a narrow little glen below Cow Castle. Follow track keeping the series of little hills on your left and continue over the March burn to take up the track at the foot of White Hill and Mitchell Hill. Follow track east to Mitchell Hill Farm.

	Grid Ref.	Distance
3.	067 339	3 ½ miles

Follow track round to the left at the farm and then take right fork to gate. Enter field and follow track across the field to forestry. From forestry follow track out to road.

4. 063 348   4 miles

Turn left onto road and follow all the way to Coulter Village Hall.

5. 025 338   7 miles

End: Coulter Village Hall.

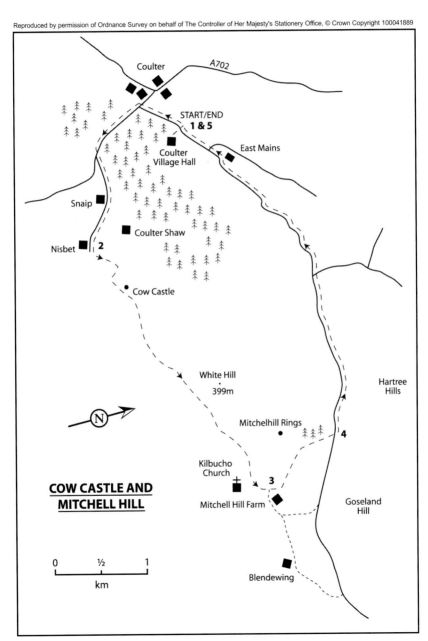

COW CASTLE AND
MITCHELL HILL

LAMINGTON, WINDGATE HOUSE AND THE DEILS'S BARN DOOR

Distance: 12 miles.

Grade: hard.

Starting point/finishing point: Lamington, car park by church.

Maps: OS Landranger 72, OS Explorer 335 and 336. Compass required.

Terrain: this route follows good tracks for most of the time however towards the end of the route the track is difficult to detect in places.

BY THE WAY

Lamington is a pretty village - a hamlet really - and it was planned that way. Lord Lamington, a Victorian improver had designed for him a village of typical cottages with gardens fringed with white picket fences and a quaint canopy of stone and slate for the village wellhead.

The only note of incongruity is the village Kirk which is an austere grey stone box. Robert Burns attended a service there and inscribed on the window, "As cauld a wind ever blew, a cauld kirk an in't but few, as cauld a minister's e'er spak, Ye's a' be het e'e r I come back". Burns' sentiments are not difficult to understand for the church also sits on an exposed knowe which catches the winds blowing up the Clyde Valley. Burns may not have found the church or the minister warm but it was welcome shelter in 1715 for 200 retreating Jacobites.

The Kirk is plain except for an ornate ancient doorway that survives from the original Norman church. The doorway is closed off and half buried but it is reasonable to assume that through this door passed Marion Braidfute, wife of William Wallace as she is Lamington's most famous daughter.

Leaving Lamington it is clear that Lord Lamington's desire for order did not limit itself to the village for he also landscaped the hillside with yew and rhododendron and dammed its burns.

From Lord Lamington's park the route crosses rather unremarkable open hillside. Ahead is a narrow steep sided pass which isn't immediately obvious. Once through the pass you emerge in the Cowgill Glen and a different world of fat pudding like hills. Once there was a whole community living here. A temporary village of wooden huts accommodated the men who built the Coulter and Cowgill dams. The settlement included a school, a mission house, a reading room and a grocery store.

Looking down the Cowgill Glen from Cowgill Rig

The reservoir road is the link between the pass and the track that climbs over the Cowgill Rig. It is from this narrow spur of land that you will get your first glimpse of Culter Fell and the jumble of peaks that surround it.

It is a steep descent to the Cowgill Reservoir and from there it is a short detour for the path to Windgate House. Windgate is now a ruin but its thick stone walls turning into a distinctive barrel-roofed byre and its internal steps that once led to an upper accommodation chamber mark this out as a bastle house. Usually these were built by tenant farmers to protect their livestock and family from marauding reivers but this one is in an unlikely and probably unsustainable location so it may have been built by a privacy seeking Laird of Lamington.

From this cool and sunless spot it is uphill towards the Deil's Barn Door. Out in the open again an indistinct path leads to Hardrig Head. The track which is known as the Peat Road, because it was used by those harvesting peat from the moors, leads back to Lamington.

THE ROUTE

	Grid Ref.	Distance
1.	978 308 (Explorer 335)	0

Start:: Lamington, car park (south end of village).Leave car park by turning right past Lamington Church and continue through hamlet to emerge at the A702. Cross the A702 and continue past row of cottages to white gate.

2. 981 310(Explorer 335) ⅓ mile

Go through white gate and wander round rhododendrons to estate road. Turn right and then immediately left to follow track above kennels. When there is open hillside on your left go through gate on the left onto open hillside and follow track uphill. Follow track through narrow pass past Cowgill Loch, eventually emerging at reservoir road.

3. 011 298(Explorer 336) 3 ½ miles

Turn left onto reservoir road and follow for about ½ mile. Take track off to the right that goes south and uphill on pronounced ridge. Follow this track beyond the forestry plantation and then follow zigzags downhill to reservoir. Turn left for Windgate House.

4. 016 272 6 ½ miles

From Windgate House return to reservoir and follow path that goes off to the left and follows Duncan Gill steeply uphill and onto hilltops. Follow track to fence and then follow fence north-west to trig point at 004 260.

5. 004 260 8 ½ miles

Continue to follow fence to Hardrig Head. From Hardrig Head follow fence and pronounced spur north and then follow hill track north west which descends past grouse buts to Bleakfield Farm. Cross stream on bridge and then follow road all the way to junction with A702. Turn right for Lamington. Alternatively follow fence west to Ewe Hill and then turn north to follow the at times indistinct Old Peat Route to large farm at Baitlaws. Join road and continue north to A702 turn right for Lamington

6. 978 308(Explorer335) 12 miles(13 miles)

End: car park, Lamington.

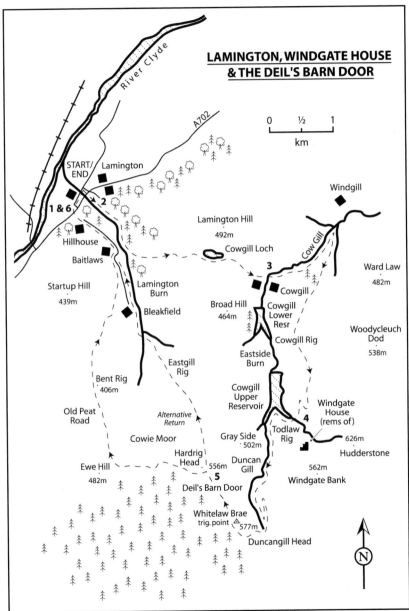

LAMINGTON, WINDGATE HOUSE & THE DEIL'S BARN DOOR

River Clyde

A702

0   ½   1
km

START/END   Lamington

Windgill

1 & 6   2

Lamington Hill
492m

Cowgill Loch

Hillhouse

Baitlaws

Ward Law
482m

3

Cowgill

Startup Hill
439m

Lamington Burn

Broad Hill
464m

Cowgill Lower Resr

Woodycleuch Dod
538m

Bleakfield

Eastgill Rig

Cowgill Rig

Eastside Burn

Bent Rig
406m

Cowgill Upper Reservoir

Windgate House (rems of)

Old Peat Road

Alternative Return

4

Cowie Moor

Gray Side
502m

Todlaw Rig

626m

Hudderstone

Hardrig Head
556m

Duncan Gill

562m

Ewe Hill
482m

5

Windgate Bank

Deil's Barn Door

Whitelaw Brae
trig. point   577m

Duncangill Head

N

THE PENTLAND ((WITH LISTINGS FOR CARNWATH,
NEWBIGGING, DOLPHINTON AND WALSTON)
ROUTES

THE PENTLAND HILLS

The Pentland Hills are most often associated with Edinburgh and it is from Edinburgh that the hills are most often climbed. However a large chunk of the eastern Pentlands lies within Clydesdale. Clydesdale's chunk is however mostly featureless moor that arcs around the secluded and relatively benevolent South Medwin Valley.

At the head of the valley is Dunsyre, a charming hamlet with a long history. The current Dunsyre Church has only been there since the 19th century but its churchyard is many hundreds of years older and has William Somervil a signatory of the National Covenant in 1638 as one of its permanent residents. Set in the wall of the church is a set of jougs - a collar that was placed around the neck of those who strayed from the path of righteousness. Close to the entrance to the church it would have been a particularly humiliating and uncomfortable punishment; the jougs were set in the wall at such a height that the wearer could neither stand up straight nor sit.

Looking across the Medwyn valley to Dunsyre Church and Dunsyre Law

This corner of the Pentlands was a particularly favoured spot for the illegal open air prayer meetings attended by Covenanters. It is a sheltered, easily overlooked location and even today the minor road from Newbigging, by the A721, to Dunsyre sees little traffic. The nearby hills and the wooded corners would have provided a means of escape were dragoons to try to arrest the worshipping Covenanters. It was here that Donald Cargill, a leading hard line Covenanter, preached his last sermon before being arrested the next morning near Thankerton by bounty hunter Irvine of Bonshawe.

Near to Dunsyre is Newholm, the home of Major Learmouth who commanded the Covenanter horsemen at the nearby Battle of Rullion Green in 1666. At Rullion Green the Covenanters suffered a heavy defeat. From then on Learmouth was a wanted man and he would elude his pursuers via a secret passage that led from his house to a steep bank of the Medwin. He was eventually betrayed by a servant and imprisoned on the Bass Rock. He is buried in the churchyard at Dolphinton.

EATING AND DRINKING
Beechwood Tearoom, Dolphinton ~ 01968 682285
Wee Bush Inn, 99 Main St, Carnwath ~ 01555 840857
China Red, 119 Main St, Carnwath ~ 01555 841212

EATING, DRINKING AND STAYING
Nestler's Hotel, Newbigging ~ 01555 840680
Old Bush Hotel, 12-16 Main St, Carnwath ~ 01555 840060

STAYING
Dunsyre Mains, Dunsyre ~ 01899810251
Walston Mansion Farmhouse, Walston ~ 01899 810338

GETTING THERE
Road - Dolphinton is reached by following the A702(T) out of Edinburgh or north from Biggar. Newholm Picnic Site by Dunsyre is reached by turning off the A721 at the Nestler's Hotel, Newbigging signed for Dunsyre. Follow road through Dunsyre and then turn right just as you enter the trees about 500 yards beyond Dunsyre.

AROUND MENDICK HILL - DOLPHINTON TO WEST LINTON

Distance: 8 ½ miles.
Grade: easy.
Starting point/finishing point: Dolphinton Station.
Maps: OS Landranger 72, OS Explorer 336 and 344.
Terrain: good tracks and quiet tarmac roads throughout.

BY THE WAY

After a meandering start the path straightens and stiffens - a sure sign that you are following a Roman road. It is also the line of the old road between Biggar, West Linton and Carlops and the latter two are still linked by it. A very evocative spot is where the old road crosses a sandstone bridge built in 1620.

On the return leg there is plenty of evidence of the presence of ancient peoples. Ahead the cultivation terraces on Dunsyre Law are very obvious as is the large Nether Cairn which sits close the path.

THE ROUTE

	Grid Ref.	Distance
1.	111 478	0

Start: Former Dolphinton Station, by the A702. Follow minor road away from A702 for 200 yards.

2.	111 479	200 yards

Turn right off minor road at right of way sign for West Linton 4 miles. Continue through gate and round to the right and follow track uphill towards white cottage.

3.	112 482	¼ mile

Continue through gate at white cottage and follow track round to the left (look out for tiny Tweed Trail signs). Continue towards stand of pine trees. Follow track past Ingraston Farm.

4.	135 513	2 ¾ miles

Eventually you encounter a crossroads. Go straight on passing the South Slipperfield cottages to the left, signed West Linton. Continue through gate and follow grassy track over old bridge. Follow track to junction with golf course road.

5.	139 517	3 ½ miles

Turn left onto golf course road, signed Garvald 3 miles, Dunsyre 5 miles, and follow through gate at North Slipperfield. Ignore track on the left at sheepfold and continue to next left at small grey building.

6.   123 517   4 ½ miles

Take left at grey building signed Dunsyre 4 miles, Boston Cottage and Crosswood 7 miles. Follow good gravel track for about ¾ mile after which it becomes a less obvious and narrower grassy track. Do not follow any of the tracks through gates but continue to follow the track above the Garvald Burn to the large house at Ferniehaugh.

7.   101 497   6 ½ miles

At Ferniehaugh go to the left away from the house past the duck pond. Continue straight on at duck pond and follow tree lined drive to Garvald Home Farm. Go round to the left at barn and follow tarmac road past The Garvald Trust (following the signs at the barn will take you to Dunsyre and not Dolphinton). Follow tarmac road all the way to T-junction opposite gravel quarry.

8.   102 484   7 ½ miles

Turn left and follow road to Dolphinton Station

9.   111 478   8 ½ miles

End: Dolphinton Station by A702.

see map p78

The 17th century bridge on the old Biggar to Edinburgh road and Mendick Hill beyond

THE COVENANTER'S GRAVE

Distance: 4 ½ miles (9 miles round trip).
Grade: moderate.
Starting point: Newholm Bridge Picnic Site.
Finishing point: Covenanter's Grave, Bleak Law.
Maps: OS Landranger 72, OS Explorer 344. Compass essential.
Terrain: Exposed, featureless and very boggy moor for the most part.

BY THE WAY

This route follows a right of way, which if it was followed to its conclusion would take you to the Crosswood Reservoir by the A70. Once at the Crosswood Reservoir the only option would be to walk back the way you had come unless you'd left a second car there before setting out.

The path is not often followed and can no longer be detected for most of its length. As a result it is a long trudge through deep heather following a compass bearing. The moor is utterly empty of landmarks and the hills lack a distinctive character so it is not a walk to attempt in mist or in bad weather. Also new rough roads, to facilitate grouse shooting, have been bulldozed across the moor, which are not yet marked on the map. This only adds to the confusion.

There is however a touching story associated with this route across the moor and in following it you'll be retracing the footsteps of a local shepherd Adam Sanderson who tried to fulfil the dying wish of a Covenanter wounded at the Battle of Rullion Green.

On 28th November 1666 Sanderson encountered the Covenanter desperately trying to get to a point from where he could see the Ayrshire hills just one last time. Sanderson offered him assistance but it was refused. The next day Sanderson found his body at Oaken Bush.

At great personal risk, as government troops would have

The Covenanter's Grave

been scouring the area for fugitives, Sanderson transported the body high onto the moors a little way short of the summit of Black Law as it is from this point you can look west between Darlees Rig and Bleak Law to the Ayrshire hills.

Archaeologists excavated the grave and found the Covenanter's well preserved body wrapped in a red cloak with two Dutch coins sewn into his collar. The original marker stone with its coded inscription now sits on the windowsill of Dunsyre Kirk.

THE ROUTE

	Grid Ref.	Distance
1.	077 478	0

Start: Newholm Bridge Picnic Site.Return to road and turn to the left. Follow road into Dunsyre. Take right signed Public Footpath, Garvald and West Linton. Follow lane past Dunsyre Mains out of Dunsyre.

2.	086 488	1 ½ miles

When road swings to the left for Easton Farm continue straight ahead onto rough track. After ½ mile you encounter a ford. Go to the left for footbridge. Resume track on far side of ford and continue through gate.

3.	095 494	2 ¼ miles

At second gate turn left off the track signed Crosswood via Covenanter's Grave 6 miles (sign facing away from you). Stick with the fence and ignore track that descends to the West Water. Eventually you encounter a stile. Cross stile and go uphill to the right through bracken. After 100 yards gap in bracken indicates path going to the left. Track is just about discernible as you stick with the top of the steep sides of the shallow valley on your left. As the valley sides relax leave the valley and go off to the right to find a wooden sighting pole with a white painted top that marks out the line of the right of way.From now on path is impossible to make out so set your compass to 336° and follow bearing across moor. You should encounter more poles and the butts on the north side of Cairn Knowe. Basically you are aiming for the end of the spur coming off Bleak Law. Eventually you encounter the track from West Linton that leads to a dam a mile away to your left.

4.	083 515	4 miles

Try to locate line of butts going up Black Law and follow almost to summit otherwise pick a route that takes you just to the left of the summit where you should be able to locate the grave marked by a large gravestone.

5.	077 523	4 ½ miles

End: Covenanter's Grave, Black Law.

see map p78

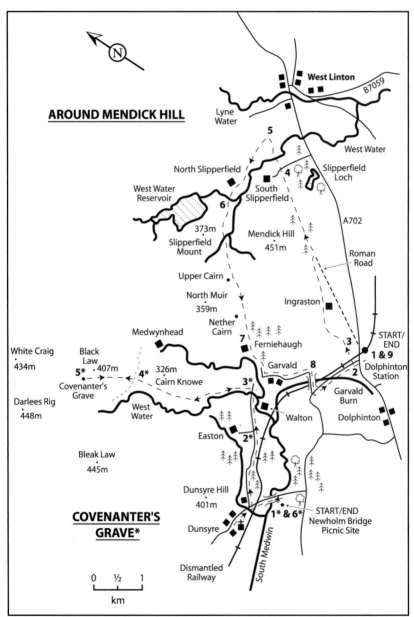

AROUND MENDICK HILL

West Linton

B7059

Lyne Water

5

West Water

North Slipperfield

4

Slipperfield Loch

West Water Reservoir

South Slipperfield

6

A702

373m

Slipperfield Mount

Mendick Hill
451m

Roman Road

Upper Cairn

North Muir
359m

Ingraston

Nether Cairn

Medwynhead

7

Ferniehaugh

START/END
1 & 9

White Craig
434m

Black Law

5* ·407m

4*

326m
Cairn Knowe

Garvald

8

3

Dolphinton Station

Covenanter's Grave

3*

2

Darlees Rig
448m

West Water

Garvald Burn

Bleak Law
445m

Walton

Dolphinton

Easton

2*

COVENANTER'S GRAVE*

Dunsyre Hill
401m

Dunsyre

1* & 6*

START/END
Newholm Bridge
Picnic Site

0   ½   1

South Medwin

km

Dismantled Railway

THE BLACK MOUNT

Distance: 5 ½ miles.
Grade: moderate/hard.
Starting point/finishing point: Newholm Bridge Picnic Site.
Maps: Landranger sheet 72, Explorer 336. Compass required.
Terrain: quiet tarmac roads, good tracks and open heathery hillside.

BY THE WAY

The Black Mount is compact in both girth and height although its steep slopes and isolated position make it look higher. The ascent is tackled via a little valley in its north flank. The valley hidden from view, was possibly the site of illegal prayer meetings held by Covenanters. This would seem to be confirmed by the feature marked on the Explorer map known as Auld Kirk Wa's - a rocky little pocket which would have provided good cover for praying Covenanters. However were anyone to inform on them they would have had little chance of escape as the valley comes to an abrupt end.

From the summit there is an excellent view to the north and east where the more shapely summits in the Pentland Hills can be easily picked out.

THE ROUTE

	Grid Ref.	Distance
1.	077 478	0

Start: Newholm Bridge Picnic Site.Return to road and turn right. Follow road to junction and turn right. Continue to follow road past Westfield Farm.

| 2. | 074 471 | 1 ½ miles |

200 yards beyond Westfield Farm turn left off the road and through gate. Follow deeply rutted track uphill and round to the left into very narrow and hidden valley.

| 3. | 079 466 | 2 miles |

Track comes to an end at small quarry. Follow grassy ramp beyond quarry. Ramp grows increasingly steep and it is loose and stony towards the top. There are many sheep tracks to the left and right that can be followed to reach the skyline. You emerge onto open hillside between Newholm Hill and Windlestraw Top.

| 4. | 081 467 | 2 ¼ miles |

Follow broad ridge to the right of Windlestraw Top to attain broad and level summit ridge. Follow fence south west to trig point at the summit.

5.   080 460   3 miles

Descend from summit in the direction of Borland Hill (west) skirting deep cleuch on the right. Descend through bracken to March Burn (steep in places) Cross burn and climb to outward path. Return by outward route.

6.   077 478   5 ½ miles

End: Newholm Bridge Picnic Site.

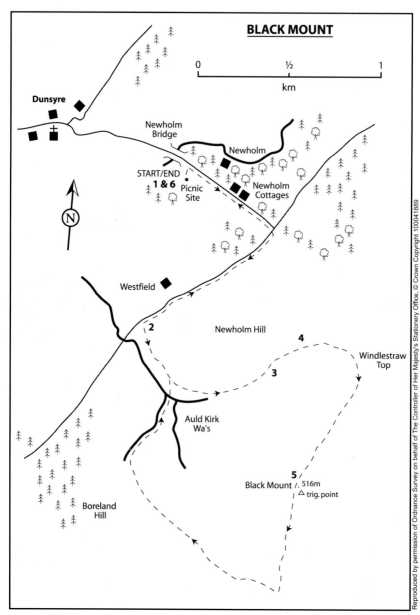

THE DOUGLAS
(WITH LISTINGS FOR LESMAHAGOW AND BLACKWOOD)
ROUTES

Old St Bride's Church, Douglas

DOUGLAS

Douglas takes its name from the family who in the 13th and 14th centuries were amongst the most powerful in Scotland and controlled most of the south-west. Douglas was the family's powerbase and consequently Douglas has a rich history that can be immediately appreciated by wandering its narrow streets.

On Main Street there is a memorial cairn to James Gavin, a tailor and Covenanter who had his ears cut off with his own shears by Bloody Claverhouse and then banished to Barbados. The lintel he carved is incorporated into the memorial.

At the centre of the village, with its 15th-century octagonal tower is St Bride's Church. The clock in the tower is reckoned to be the oldest working clock in Scotland and was presented to the church in 1565 by Mary Queen of Scots. In the spirit of the Douglas family motto 'Never Behind' it chimes three minutes ahead of every hour.

A sign on the gate to the churchyard will tell you where to obtain the key to the church and once inside you can peer through the glass set in the floor at the casket containing the heart of 'The Good' Sir James Douglas who was Robert the Bruce's right hand man in the fight with England; the other casket contains the heart of Sir Archibald Douglas who died in 1513.

Sir James promised the dying Bruce that he would take his heart to the Holy Land so that in some way Bruce's desire to fight in a crusade could be fufilled. Sir James was killed in Spain in 1330 at the hands on the Moors, en route to the Holy Land. His time worn tomb and those of other Douglasses are set against the walls. A beautifully carved and slightly spooky marble effigy of Lucy Elizabeth, Countess of Home sits on the altar.

Not far from St Bride's is the pointing statue of the Earl of Angus. He is pointing to the field in which the Angus regiment later known as the Cameronian's was first raised in 1689. The Cameronians take their name from Richard Cameron, a hard line and prominent Covenanter who was behind the treasonable Declaration of Sanquhar of 1680. It was also in 1680 that Cameron was killed in a skirmish with Claverhouse's dragoons at Aird's Moss in Ayrshire.

It was in the building across the narrow road from St. Bride's, once known as the Sun Inn, which was at the time of the Covenanters the tollbooth, that 'Bloody' Claverhouse rested after the battle on Aird's Moss with the severed head and hands of Richard Cameron. The Sun Inn which was built in 1621 is Douglas's oldest intact building and it is now a private residence.

EATING AND DRINKING
Douglas (01555 -)
Douglas Arms Hotel, 54 Ayr Road ~ 851322
Cross Keys, 68 Main Street ~ 851435
Spice of Life, 15 Main St ~ 850200
Crossburn Service Station Café, 56 Ayr Road ~ 851043
Cairn Lodge Services, Happendon ~ 851177

Blackwood, Kirkmuirhill and Lesmahagow (01555 -)
The Fountain Resturant, 9 Abbeygreen, Lesmahagow ~ 893237
Azzuri Bistro Italiano, 14 Abbeygreen ~ 895921
Pardesi Daba, 18 Abbeygreen, Lesmahagow ~ 890024
Jerry's Chinese Cuisine, 12 Priory Road ~ 890088
The Star Inn, 515 Carlisle Road (2 miles south of Lesmahagow) ~ 892293

STAYING
Douglas(01555 -)
Crossburn Caravan and Camping Park, Ayr Road ~ 851043

Dallmartin Cottage, 2 Cairnhouses Road ~ 851433
Blackwood, Kirkmuirhill and Lesmahagow (01555 -)
Dykecroft Farm, Kirkmuirhill ~ 892226
Hopehill Cottage, 22 Vere Road, Blackwood ~ 893249
The Kerse B&B, The Kerse, Lesmahagow ~ 894545

GETTING THERE

Road - Douglas is cut in two by the Edinburgh to Ayr road the A70. The village also lies two miles west of junction 12 of the M74 and so it is a particularly easy place to reach.

Bus - There is an hourly service (Service 9) Monday - Saturday from Lanark Interchange to Douglas and on to Glespin; the Sunday service is every three hours. Service X50 leaves Hamilton Bus Station every two hours, Monday - Saturday for Lesmahagow, Douglas and Glespin.
For all public transport enquiries call Traveline 0870 608 2 608

The first four routes in this chapter are being developed by the Douglas Valley Rural Action Partnership and will eventually be way-marked.

HAGSHAW HILL

Distance: 4 miles (8 miles round trip).
Grade: moderate.
Starting point: Old St Bride's Church Main St entrance, Douglas.
Finishing point: summit trig point Hagshaw Hill.
Maps: OS Landranger 72, OS Explorer 335
Terrain: quiet tarmac road and loose gravel access road.

BY THE WAY

It is unlikely that you'd climb Hagshaw Hill were it not for 26 wind turbines on its summit and the access road that removes the need to struggle with the rough and tussocky terrain.

The wind turbines are hidden from view until you are well up the hill and contrary to popular perceptions you cannot hear them until you are right underneath them. Rather anomalously the view on the way up is of a landscape scarred by open cast mining and it is in this context that the wind farm isn't such an eyesore.

In all there are 26 wind turbines each with a generating capacity of 600kW giving a total generating capacity of 15.6MW which is enough to supply power to 10,000 homes.

THE ROUTE

	Grid Ref.	Distance
1.	836 309	0

Start: Old St Bride's Church. Follow Main St to the right out to Ayr Road (A70). Turn right and follow Ayr Road out of Douglas.

2.	833 304	½ mile

Turn right for Douglas West (Station Road) and follow road uphill to Douglas West.

3.	821 310	1 ½ mile

At the road end at Douglas West continue straight on through gate and follow gravel access road to summit where there are a couple of loops to be explored.

4.	793 308	4 miles

End: summit trig point, Hagshaw Hill.

see map p86

Wind turbines on Hagshaw Hill

WINDROW WOOD

Distance: 4 ½ miles.
Grade: easy.
Starting point/finishing point: Old St Bride's Church, Douglas.
Maps: OS Landranger 72, OS Explorer Sheet 335.
Terrain: good tracks and paths throughout.

BY THE WAY

The Windrow Wood was turned over to unemployed weavers at the end of the last century to build footpaths for local people to enjoy. A century later it is still a delightful walk up a shallow glen filled with deciduous native woodland.

THE ROUTE

	Grid Ref.	Distance
1.	836 309	0

Start: Old St Bride's Church. Turn left away from the village centre in the direction of the Cameronian Monument and Castle Dangerous. Continue past Crabtree St and the Colonel's Entry.

2.	837 311	400 yards

Turn left onto footpath between row of white cottages and the West Lodge. Follow footpath to recreation ground and then to blue bridge beyond. Cross bridge and continue to junction with broader track.

3.	834 313	½ mile

Turn left and follow track for about 1 mile, going straight over Station Road.

4.	825 299	1 ¾ miles

At Windrow Cottage go to the right and continue through gate. Follow track into the woods. Track narrows and follows burn upstream.

5.	816 296	2 ½ miles

Eventually you come to two footbridges. Use the downstream bridge to cross as the other is dilapidated. However take up the path that leads away from the other bridge and follow it as it hooks round and zig-zags up the side of the valley.

6.	815 296	2 ½ miles

When you encounter the conifer plantation turn to the left and follow track which eventually enters the trees. After a short distance in the trees turn left at junction of tracks and then leave the forest through gate at Windrow Cottage. Retrace outward route to Douglas.

7.	836 309	4 ½ miles

End: Old St Bride's Church.

see map p86

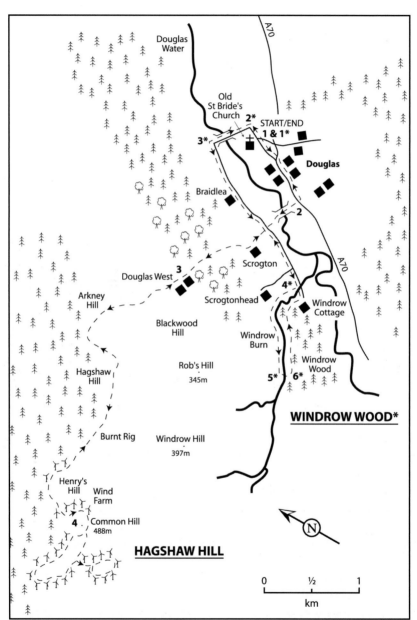

Douglas Water

A70

Old
St Bride's
Church 2*
3* START/END
1 & 1*
Douglas

Braidlea

Scrogton

2

A70

Douglas West 3
Arkney
Hill 4*
Scrogtonhead
Windrow
Cottage

Blackwood
Hill
Windrow
Burn

Rob's Hill
345m
Windrow
Wood
Hagshaw
Hill 5* 6*

WINDROW WOOD*

Burnt Rig Windrow Hill
397m

Henry's
Hill Wind
Farm
Common Hill 4
488m

HAGSHAW HILL

N

0   ½   1

km

CASTLE LOOP AND CURLY BRAE

Distance: 5 miles.
Grade: easy.
Starting point/finishing point: St Bride's Church, Douglas.
Maps: OS Landranger 72, OS Explorer 335.
Terrain: good tracks throughout.

BY THE WAY

The Adam designed castle built in 1757 is no longer and although it is more than sixty years since its demise its presence can still be felt through the ostentatious bridges, ornamental lochs and the landscape of loosely planted mature trees.

The Cameronian Monument

The 18th century castle was demolished in 1938 when its structure was found to have become unsafe as a result of local mining activity. There are no tangible remains of the Adams' castle however a small part of the 13th century castle is to be found on top of a grassy knoll. The castle is often referred to as Castle Dangerous because it was Douglas Castle and the ruthless actions of 'Good' Sir James Douglas, who surprised the English troops occupying his castle while they were at church on Palm Sunday 1304, that inspired Sir Walter Scott's book *Castle Dangerous*.

On your left just before the ruined tower of the old Douglas Castle is a fenced off area within which is a monument to the disbanding of the Cameronian Regiment in 1968. The monument remains a focus for old Cameronians and each year on the Sunday closest to 14th May (known as Cameronian Sunday) they hold a conventicle, posting sentries as they would have done during the Killing Times to look out for approaching dragoons.

Most of the grass grown founds that can be detected are those of nissan huts that housed troops when the estate became an army vehicle depot during World War II. Also stationed here during the war were the Polish Cavalry, however they spent their time here under canvas; three monuments that commemorate their time here are to be found opposite the West Lodge.

At the half way point the brick chimney breasts poking out of the woodland undergrowth are all that remain of the German Prisoner of War Camp. Sixty years ago it is likely that you would have had to share your walk in the woods with hundreds of prisoners making their way from the camp to the Douglas West pit baths for their weekly wash.

THE ROUTE

	Grid Ref.	Distance
1.	836 309	0

Start: Old St Bride's Church.Turn left in the direction of the Cameronian Monument and Castle Dangerous. Continue past Crabtree St and follow road round to the left (do not follow the Colonel's Entry) to West Lodge.

2.	838 312	400 yards

Just beyond West Lodge the un-surfaced estate road forks. Take the right, signed 'Right of Way, Douglas Castle'.

3.	832 316	½ mile

At far side of the loch go to the right away from the loch in the direction of the Cameronian Monument. 100 yards further on is remaining tower of Douglas Castle /Castle Dangerous

4.	842 317	¾ mile

Just before the Castle turn to the left and descend to bridge. Cross bridge and follow road up to Gardens House where you go round to the right and continue through sheepfold. Follow long straight track for about 1 mile to edge of conifer plantation.

5.   852 332   2 ¼ miles
Continue straight on into conifer plantation on a track that is at first overgrown. Follow track to within touching distance of the M74 and then away from the motorway until you encounter a clearing towered over by tall pines.

6.   840 328   3 ½ miles
In the clearing turn left and follow track downhill to barrier and gate. Go through both to emerge on outward route between Gardens House and sheepfold. Go towards house. Return to bridge and retrace the outward route back to castle and the Cameronian Monument.

7.   832 316   4 ¼ miles
Just beyond the Cameronian Monument take the track that goes to the right. You then leave this track to follow the narrow footpath which follows the shore of the loch. Leave the loch side to cross stile at West Lodge. From West Lodge follow outward route to St Bride's.

8.   836 309   5 miles
End: St. Bride's Church.

see map p91

MOUNTAIN DRIVE

Distance: 4 miles.
Grade: moderate.
Starting point/finishing point: St Bride's Church, Douglas.
Maps: OS Landranger 72, OS Explorer 335.
Terrain: good tracks and footpaths throughout.

BY THE WAY

There is not much to say about this route other than it offers good exercise. Locals get the New Year off to a good start by walking the route. Although it should be said that exercise is not their primary concern rather it is the water in the Pagie Burn which is apparently very pure and very good with whisky. Fortified with a dram or two the New Year walkers entertain each other with poetry and yarns.

The occasional views of the wind farm on Hagshaw Hill and Cairn Table in the west are good but most of the time the view is obscured by thick conifer plantations so this is a good route for when the weather is inclement as it is generally sheltered.

THE ROUTE

	Grid Ref.	Distance
1.	836 309	0

Start: Old St Bride's Church, Main St entrance. Go straight over onto Clyde Road and follow to The Loaning. Turn right onto The Loaning and follow uphill to Ayr Road (A70).

2.   837 307   250 yards

Cross Ayr Road (TAKE CARE - RESRTICTED VIEW OF TRAFFIC COMING FROM RIGHT) and follow Springhill Road past children's play park. Follow Springhill Road uphill.

3.   840 304   ½ mile

When Springhill Road swings to the right to become Glebe Road continue straight ahead onto rough road. Follow rough road uphill to conifer plantation.

4.   843 298   1 mile

Just as you enter the conifer plantation take the right and follow track into trees. Follow this track for about 1 mile.

5.   832 289   2 miles

Descend to junction with another track and turn to the right and continue descent for about 250 yards.

6.   829 292   2 ¼ miles

Take easy to miss right turn which leads you out of the trees and along the edge of a field. Follow to Midtown Farm.

7   833 296   2 ¾ miles

Go to the left at Midtown Farm and descend to A70.

8.   831 298   3 miles

Either follow grass verge along A70 for about 200 yards before crossing to footpath on other side of A70 or cross to cemetery and make your way through the cemetery to an exit away to your right to join footpath into Douglas. Follow footpath to Douglas Arms Hotel where you turn left along Main Street to return to St Bride's Church.

9.   836 309   4 miles

End: Old St Bride's Church.

CASTLE LOOP & CURLY BRAE

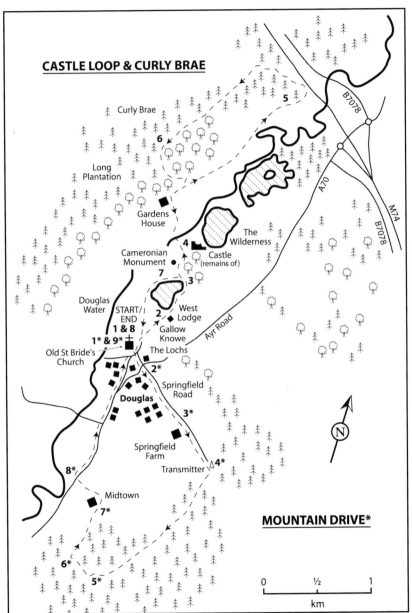

MOUNTAIN DRIVE*

CAIRN KINNEY

Distance: 3 miles.

Grade: moderate.

Starting point/finishing point: Glentaggart road end.

Maps: OS Landranger 72 (recommended), OS Explorer 335, 328, 329. Compass required.

Terrain: good tracks and open hillside.

Getting there: Follow the A70 to Glespin then take the turning for Crawfordjohn. At first T-junction turn right and then after 200 yards turn right again and follow for two miles to road end

BY THE WAY

Cairn Kinney's trig point is a rare landmark in a large tract of rather anonymous moor that stretches from the Douglas Water to the Nith in the south. Cairn Kinney itself is no more than a swelling in the moor but it is sufficiently high for you to revel in the splendid isolation and emptiness of the moor.

The walk can be extended by starting out from Glespin and returning to Glespin via Auchendaff and the footpath that follows the Kennox Water. This return route is however very boggy and is best tackled when the ground is frozen or it hasn't rained for some time.

THE ROUTE

	Grid Ref.	Distance
1.	793 235	0

Start: Glentaggart road end.From the road end descend to the left, cross bridge and follow track off in the direction of Shawhead Farm.

2.	786 223	1 mile

When track forks take left and climb uphill. When track turns right and levels out take off uphill following the rising ground to Cairn Kinney's summit trig point.

3.	785 215	2 miles

From trig point descend to return to the track. Ensure that the plantation at Shawhead Farm is on your left. Turn right off the track and descend through gate to the edge of the plantation. Continue through gate and go towards the farm. Avoid the farmyard and pass the farm on the left. Join track beyond farm and follow to Glentaggart road end.

4.	793 235	3 miles

End: Glentaggart road end.

see map p94

THE KERSE

Distance: less than 3 miles.

Grade: easy.

Starting point/finishing point: visitor car park.

Maps: OS Landranger 72, OS Explorer 335.

Terrain: good paths and grassy lanes.

Getting there:

Northbound - leave the M74 at junction 10 and turn right over the M74. At the next roundabout take the second exit. Turn to the left and follow rough road and tree-lined avenue for about 500 yards. Parking spaces are the on the left.

Southbound - leave the M74 at junction 9. At the end of the slip road turn right and follow the road to roundabout. Take left at roundabout and follow directions as for northbound.

BY THE WAY

The intensely pleasant walking through the trees by the River Nethan is being developed and extended by a Forestry Commission project. The project seeks to build upon the remnants of native woodland with a huge tree planting programme. There is a myriad of paths to follow and excellent picnic potential. The walk starts to the left of the large brown bungalow just a little further on from the car park.

no map

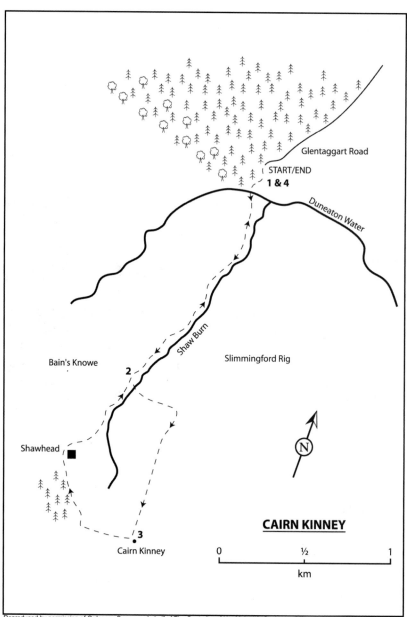

Glentaggart Road

START/END
1 & 4

Duneaton Water

Shaw Burn

Bain's Knowe

Slimmingford Rig

2

Shawhead

N

3

Cairn Kinney

CAIRN KINNEY

0 ½ 1
km

THE LOWTHER (WITH LISTINGS FOR ABINGTON,
CRAWFORD, CRAWFORDJOHN, LEADHILLS AND WANLOCKHEAD)
ROUTES

Lowther Hill, Green Lowther and the village of Leadhills

THE LOWTHER HILLS

Mention the Lowther Hills and most people will respond with a puzzled look. Describe them as the Leadhills and the same people will respond with a spark of recognition. Leadhills is in fact a Lowther village but it is possibly the best name for this range of hills because for the last two millennia at least these hills have been mined for their minerals and especially lead.

It was with this in mind that the hills were, in the 19th century, re-christened by the Rev Moir Porteous as 'Gods Own Treasure House in Scotland'. However the treasure to be found in the Leadhills and in particular gold was not extracted for God but for Elizabeth I by Bevis Bulmer and for the Scottish Crown jewels. Later it was the Earl of Hopetoun and the Duke of Buccleuch that benefited from the deposits of mainly lead but also of zinc.

The piles of spoil, the old railway tracks, the ruined mine buildings and the extensive network of ancient tracks do not detract from the bleak wildness or the beauty of the Lowthers. Rather the mining detritus and the villages of Wanlockhead and Leadhills redolent of this era are a visible layer of human endeavour that combines with the mysterious landscape of steep cleuchs and sun starved valleys to provide the visitor with a compelling and fascinating experience.

The Lowther Hills may be low and rounded but the extensive views of rolling hills can still induce awe as can a journey that takes in the glaciated Dalveen valley and the narrow and steep sided Mennock Pass.

The rounded nature of the Lowthers means that dangerous precipices are rarely encountered but the weather can be ferocious and snow showers are frequent from October onwards. They are not therefore the place for inexperienced navigators as you could wander lost for long enough to place you in peril.

ABINGTON
Abington is a surprisingly pleasant village and seems to suffer few ill effects from being sandwiched between the West Coast Main Line and the M74. The village was created by the politically influential Colebrooks in the 19th century and the overall impression is one of tidy uniformity.

CRAWFORD
Crawford is an ancient settlement, the Romans built a large fort nearby and Robert II elevated it to a burgh of barony in 1370, giving the village the right to hold markets.

Strung out along what used to be the main road south Crawford has always been a well used staging post. The Crawford Inn had many famous patrons including Sir Robert Peel, Henry, the Duke of Bordeaux (rightful heir to the French crown) and Prince Louis Napoleon Bonaparte.

With the arrival of the railway the village became a popular tourist destination, even although it sits at over 900 feet above sea level and is known for being a very cold spot. Easily reached from both Glasgow and Edinburgh it was popular day trip for anglers and those wishing to picnic by the Clyde.

LEADHILLS
Leadhills is still easily identified as a mining village even though it is 70 years since serious mining ceased. A factory village with no grand plan it has an endearing informality and feels little changed. Terraced villas and cottages in pastel colours line un-surfaced roads.

The world renowned mathematician James Stirling was a popular and forward thinking mine manager who improved the efficiency of the mines and the lot of the miners considerably. Stirling with the help of the Pentland Poet Allan Ramsay, a native of Leadhills, instituted what is regarded to be Scotland's oldest subscription library in 1741. The library is on Main Street and still in use today as a reference library.

Stirling was responsible for many reforms including the reduction of working hours, days off, mine ventilation and a local version of National Insurance which may account for how one local resident, John Taylor, managed to live for 137 years; well according to his gravestone anyway.

It may have been Stirling's legacy of encouraging the miners to value and seek education that motivated local lad William Symington to become an engineer and be the first person to design and build a boat propelled by steam engine. He was however ahead of his time and died penniless.

Near the centre of the village on a slight promontory, is the curfew bell. Suspended from pyramidal supports it carries the date of 1770. The bell would peel at the change of shifts but now it is only rung to bring in the New Year and the occasional emergency.

WANLOCKHEAD

Wanlockhead, Scotland's highest village sits in a hollow just over the watershed in Nithsdale. The houses rise up the sides but don't quite manage to spill out. On sunny days the village is a very appealing place but in the winter very cold air sinks into the hollow and heavy snow is common as early as October.

Wanlockhead is like Leadhills a former lead mining village but here the experience is more formal. There is a Lead Mining Museum which includes an opportunity to go down the Loch Nell Mine, pan for gold, browse the miner's library and experience a typical miner's cottage.

It is however enough to wander the old track beds to view the old beam engine that pumped water from the mines still sitting in its place.

EATING AND DRINKING

Colebrook Arms, 7 Main Street, Crawfordjohn ~ 01864 504239
Hopetoun Arms Hotel, 37 Main Street, Leadhills ~ 01659 74234
Museum of Leadmining, Goldscaur Row, Wanlockhead ~ 01659 74387

STAYING

Days Inn, M74 Junction 13, Abington ~ 01864 502782
Abington Hotel, Carlisle Road, Abington ~01864 502467
Heatherghyll Motel, 20 Carlisle Road, Crawford ~ 01864 502641
Crawford Arms Hotel, 111 Carlisle Road, Crawford ~ 01864 502641

Lyndsey Towers, 30 Carlisle Road, Crawford ~ 01864 502855
Holmlands B&B, 22 Carlisle Road, Crawford ~ 01864 502 753
Rob Roy Caravan Park, Carlisle Road, Crawford ~ 01524 64829
Meadowfoot Cottage, 6 Gowanbank, Leadhills ~ 01659 74369
Wanlockhead Youth Hostel, Lotus Lodge, Wanlockhead ~01659 74252

GETTING THERE

Road - Leave the M74 at junction 13 and follow signs for Abington. To continue to Crawford follow the A702 south from Abington. To reach Leadhills and Wanlockhead turn right just to the south of Abington and follow the B797 south. From Edinburgh follow the A702 south via Biggar.

Bus - **Stuart's Coaches** operate 4 services daily, Monday - Saturday from Lanark Interchange to Sanquhar which calls at Abington, Crawford, Leadhills and Wanlockhead.
MacEwan's Coach Services operate 3 services daily, Monday - Saturday, and 1 service on a Sunday, from Biggar Corn Exchange to Dumfries which calls at Abington and Crawford.
For all public transport enquiries call Traveline 0870 608 2 608

Beam engine and pit shaft, Wanlockhead.

AROUND RAGGENGILL AND CASTLE HILL

Distance: 7 miles.

Grade: moderate.

Starting point/finishing point: Camps Reservoir Road.

Maps: OS Landranger 72, OS Explorer 329.

Terrain: good tracks that are soft only in a few places and quiet back roads.

Getting there: in Crawford turn off at the dilapidated Post Horn Hotel and the Mercat Cross and cross the railway line on narrow bridge. Follow road over Clyde and through Midlock Farm. At fork in the road beyond Midlock Farm take left and follow road to starting point.

BY THE WAY

The West Coast Main Line and the M74 along with the Clyde squeeze through a narrowing in the valley at Abington. This modern day route however was much too scary for the Romans who feared ambush in the narrow valley.

The Romans chose to detour around Raggengill Hill and climb high above the valley. This walk joins up with the Roman's route and their road can still be felt solidly underfoot.

On the downhill side the hillside on your right sweeps steeply up to Arbory Hill Fort. Boldly visible the Iron Age fort was occupied for about 1000 years from about 600BC to 400AD so it would have been in use when the Romans were making their way below. The fort is a formidable viewpoint and worth investigating.

Difficult to detect in the trees by the roadside near the end of the walk is the mossy ruin of Crawford Castle or as it sometimes known Lindsay Tower. The castle was at one time a royal castle and was in 1537 the venue for a dinner in honour of the French Ambassador who was in Scotland because James V was about to marry his first wife Magdalene of France. At the meal the guests were presented with cups full of gold bonnet pieces, the gold having been mined from the nearby Crawford Moor.

Despite the proximity of the motorway and railway to the return route it is very peaceful and there are many good picnic spots.

THE ROUTE

	Grid Ref.	Distance
1.	971 222	0

Start: Camps Reservoir Road at access road to Normangill Farm. Go towards Normangill Farm.

2.	972 226	¼ mile

Just before the farm turn left over wooden bridge and continue past row of houses. Keeping the dyke on your right continue through the fields until you reach the T-shaped forestry plantation.

3.	961 225	1 mile

At plantation step over 2 fences and then take up path that goes to the left of the square plantation and follow uphill. The Roman road appears to your left - you can cross the dip to join it or join it at the top of the pass. Follow the Roman road through the pass and down the far side to the minor road by the former Hickory Golf course.

4.	938 233	2 ¾ miles

Join the road and go to the left (south) continuing past the turning for Abington. Follow this minor road with the railway line close by to a T-junction.

5.	952 414	5 ¼ miles

Turn left at T-junction continue past Crawford Castle and follow through Midlock Farm. Take the left at fork in road beyond Midlock and follow road to starting point.

6.	971 222	7 miles

End: Camps Reservoir Road at access road to Normangill Farm.

see map p102

ROME HILL AND TEWSGILL HILL

Distance: 5 ¾ miles.

Grade: moderate.

Starting point/finishing point: Camps Reservoir Road at access road to Normangill Farm.

Maps: OS Landranger 72 (recommended), OS Explorer 335 and 329.

Terrain: good tracks and open hillside over which the going is fairly easy. On the way down, however, over Crannies Hill the grass is very tussocky and the going difficult.

Getting there: see Raggengill Hill route.

BY THE WAY

These two hills are sufficiently high to offer extensive views of the Clyde Valley, the deep cleuchs on the hills' southern slopes give them character and yet the ascent is relatively gentle. All in all these hills offer a hill top experience in return for little effort.

THE ROUTE

	Grid Ref.	Distance
1.	971 222	0

Start: Camps Reservoir Road at access road to Normangill Farm. Go towards Normangill Farm.

2.	972 226	¼ mile

Just before the farm turn left over wooden bridge and continue past row of houses. Keeping the dyke on your right continue through the fields until you reach the T-shaped forestry plantation.

3.	961 225	1 mile

At plantation step over 2 fences and then take up path that goes to the left of the square plantation and follow uphill.

4.	951 231	1 ¾ miles

At the top of the pass turn right (NE) uphill. Initially it is quite steep and there are no views. As hillside lies back drift towards stone dyke away to your left and follow to crumbling summit trig point.

5.	962 238	2 ½ miles

From trig point follow dyke in an easterly direction into the dip between Tewsgill and Hawkswood. Continue to follow dyke (reduced to its founds) to summit cairn of Hawkswood Hill. Follow fence on to the summit of Rome Hill - summit cairn 50 yards from fence.

6.	981 242	3 ¾ miles

Descend in a south-easterly direction skirting around the deep cleuch that contains the Normangill Burn. Continue via Crannies Hill (marked on Explorer Map only). Aim for the wood that marks out Normangill Farm. Lower down pick up grassy track and follow through gates and past farm. Return to reservoir road

7.   971 222   5 ¾ miles

End: Camps Reservoir Road at access road to Normangill Farm.

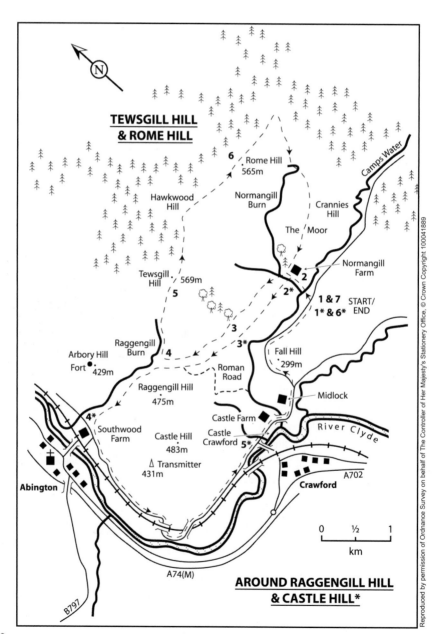

TEWSGILL HILL
& ROME HILL

AROUND RAGGENGILL HILL
& CASTLE HILL*

COOMB DOD

Distance: 9 miles (8 miles).

Grade: hard.

Starting point/finishing point: public road end, Camps Reservoir.

Maps: OS Landranger 72 (recommended), OS Explorer 329, 330, 336. Compass required.

Terrain: road around reservoir has a good surface. On the open hillside the going is good but there are large areas of peat hags that have to be negotiated near the summit of Coomb Dod.

Getting there: follow directions for Raggengill Hill walk and then continue for a further 1 ½ miles to the end of the public road.

In the hills around the Camps Reservoir

BY THE WAY

You are not far along the road from Crawford to the dam that holds back the Camps Reservoir before you are completely enveloped in hills. The dam which blends well with its surroundings was built by German PoWs during the First World War before the Geneva Convention banned such exploitation of captive soldiers. You can still detect the track bed of the railway running alongside the road that carried construction materials for the dam.

The dam and the road that follows the shore of the reservoir provides an easy start before you either follow the Grains Burn or head directly up Coomb Dod over the Backwater Rig. Coomb Dod is an unassuming outlier of Culter Fell from where you can look south across the Tweed Valley to the much higher and rougher Moffat Hills.

At the very end of the descent from North Black Dod look out for the petrifying spring that is marked on the map. The spring water is so high in minerals that it supposedly solidifies as it emerges from the ground. Apparently local people used to use the water from this spring as a food preservative. The spring is marked out by the surrounding patch of very green grass.

THE ROUTE

	Grid Ref.	Distance
1.	994 225	0

Start: public road end, Camps Reservoir.Descend towards group of buildings at the foot of the dam. Turn right at the large blue barn and follow the tarmac road to the top of the dam.

2.	001 224	¼ mile

Turn left over the top of the dam and then follow gravel road along the shore of the reservoir to Grains at the north end of the reservoir.

3.	014 239	1 ¾ mile

EITHER - continue north from Grains following the Grains Burn upstream to beyond felled forestry and cross burn to strike uphill following an indistinct grassy track up a broad shoulder to summit of Coomb Dod.**OR** follow grassy track that goes steeply uphill just before Grains Cottage and continue climbing to summit over Backwater Rig to summit of Coomb Dod.

4.	046 238	4 ¾ miles(3 ¾ miles)

Follow fence south from summit of Coomb Dod and then south-west over Culter Cleuch Shank (broad track from this point will take you to the shore of the reservoir at Camps Knowe Wood). Continue to North Black Dod and descend obvious track that services shooting butts. Join track at the foot of the hill and follow to reservoir.

5.	016 216	8 miles(7 miles)

At junction with rough road that circles reservoir turn left and follow rough road to dam. Return to road end.

6.	994 225	9 miles(8 miles)

End: public road end.

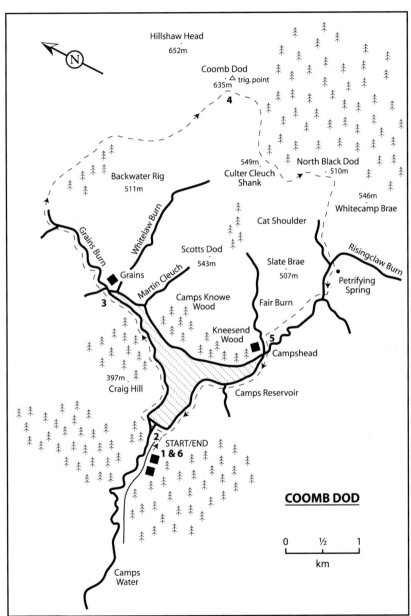

Hillshaw Head
652m

Coomb Dod
635m · △ trig. point
4

North Black Dod
549m · 510m
Culter Cleuch
Shank

546m
Whitecamp Brae

Backwater Rig
511m

Whitelaw Burn

Grains Burn

Cat Shoulder

Scotts Dod
543m ·

Slate Brae
507m

Risingclaw Burn

Grains

Martin Cleuch

Petrifying
Spring

3

Camps Knowe
Wood

Fair Burn

Kneesend
Wood

Campshead
5

397m ·
Craig Hill

Camps Reservoir

2
START/END
1 & 6

COOMB DOD

0   ½   1

km

Camps
Water

GLENOCHAR BASTLE HOUSE AND FERMTOUN TRAIL

Distance: less than two miles.

Grade: easy.

Starting point/finishing point: trail car park by A702..

Maps: OS Landranger 78, OS Explorer 329.

Terrain: initially the route is very boggy but the going improves as you go round.

Getting there: follow the A702 south from junction 14 of M74. Glenochar is three miles to the south of Elvanfoot.

BY THE WAY

Looking up Glenochar to Dun Law from the bastle house.

Bastle is derived from the French word bastille meaning 'strong' and therefore a bastle house is a strong house or more specifically a fortified house. The characteristics of a bastle house are very thick walls, a barrel roofed ground floor chamber for valuable livestock, tiny windows, an internal staircase that leads to the upper family rooms and slate roofs to render them fireproof. They were built in the 16th and 17th centuries by 'bunnet' lairds, that is tenant farmers with large flocks or herds who lived in fear of marauding reivers. The remains of bastle houses are to found throughout Northumberland and Scottish Borders but it was only recently that bastle houses were known to have been built as far north as Clydesdale

Often bastle houses were surrounded by a ferm toun (farm town) the occupants of which were unfortunately not as well protected as the laird and his livestock. Glenochar is a particularly good example of a ferm toun and contains lots of evocative details such as the roads between houses, graffiti, drainage ditches and fireplaces. The trail through the ferm toun has become a little neglected but the information boards still provide an excellent insight into 16th century life.

LOUSIE WOOD LAW

Distance: 5 miles.

Grade: hard.

Starting point/finishing point: Glenochar Bastle House and Fermtoun Trail car park by A702.

Maps: OS Landranger 78, OS Explorer 329. Compass required.

Terrain: a boggy start but the going improves beyond the Glenochar Trail. Mainly open hillsides of short grass and heather.

Getting there: see Glenochar Trail.

BY THE WAY

The Glenochar bastle house and ferm toun trail provides some early interest but it will be the view up Glenochar to the scooped face of Dun Law that will draw you on. The nature of Dun Law and Lousie Wood Law is not too dissimilar to that of nearby Lowther Hill but climbing them is enhanced by the lack of telecom paraphernalia on the hill tops.

The slopes in and out of the Little Windgate Hass between Dun Law and Lousie Wood Law is probably about as steep as a grassy hillside can be and care should be exercised.

THE ROUTE

	Grid Ref.	Distance
1.	951 137	0

Start: Glenochar Trail car park by A702.Follow the white markers that mark out the trail away from the car park. When the trail goes to the right continue straight on towards the head of the glen following a path to the left of the levee (neither marked on map). Skirt around the base of Doddin Hill and then climb to col between Doddin Hill and Dun Law.

2.	935 134	1 mile

When you hit the fence in the col follow it uphill over Kneesend. Towards the top leave the fence and make your way to summit of Dun Law.

3.	916 136	2 miles

From the summit of Dun Law follow the fence north east over White Law and then very steeply downhill into the Little Windgate Hass. Follow the fence out of the Hass to the summit trig point of Lousie Wood Law.

4.	932 153	3 ½ miles

Descend from summit of Lousie Wood to the south east over Coupland Gair. Descend broad grassy ridge into Glenochar and make your way over to rejoin the trail. Following the trail either to left or right return to the car park.

5	951 137	5 miles

End: Start: Glenochar Trail car park by A702.

see map p108

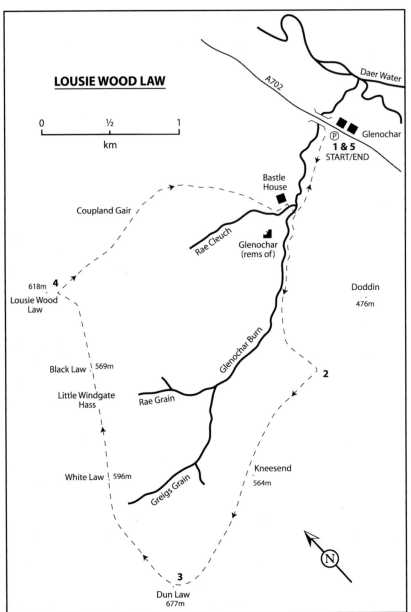

LOUSIE WOOD LAW

0 ½ 1

km

Daer Water

A702

�(P) Glenochar

1 & 5
START/END

Bastle
House

Coupland Gair

Rae Cleuch

Glenochar
(rems of)

Doddin
476m

618m **4**
Lousie Wood
Law

Glenochar Burn

Black Law ¦ 569m

2

Little Windgate
Hass

Rae Grain

Kneesend
564m

White Law ¦ 596m

Greigs Grain

N

3
Dun Law
677m

LOWTHER HILL AND GREEN LOWTHER

Lowther Hill and Green Lowther are not surprisingly the highest points in the Lowther Hills. Lowther Hill straddles the watershed between Nithsdale and Clydesdale and as a result it was seen rather bizarrely as a no-mans land and therefore a suitable place to bury 'undesirables' such as suicides and those who had been hanged as criminals. The effort to get the bodies here must have been considerable and in a further irony the carts used to transport them were abandoned on the hillside as they were now cursed by their final purpose.

Lowther Hill and Green Lowther are easily picked out on the horizon by the telecommunications paraphernalia on their summits. In particular Lowther Hill is topped by a large golf ball shaped radar station that can be picked out from miles around.

There has been a radar station on the summit of Lowther Hill since radar was developed during the Battle of Britain in World War II. The station was part of the original war time Gee chain - a low frequency radio navigation aid. Until relatively recently the radar station was manned round the clock and the maintenance teams who lived in huts at the summit were frequently snowed in for a week at a time.

The radar station is served by a tarmac road from Wanlockhead. The road is now closed to all but maintenance traffic, however in the late fifties and throughout the sixties the road was used to facilitate skiing on Lowther Hill. At the height of its popularity there were 400 people a day skiing on Lowther Hill and ski hire and lessons were available. An engine that was used to power a ski tow can still be seen sitting not far below the summit away to the left of the road.

LOWTHER HILL AND GREEN LOWTHER FROM LEADHILLS

Distance: 8 ½ miles.
Grade: moderate.
Starting point/finishing point: car park by Leadhills Primary School.
Maps: OS Landranger 71, OS Explorer 329. Compass required.
Terrain: good tracks, deep heather and tarmac roads closed to traffic.

BY THE WAY

It is probably more trouble than it's worth to avoid the radar road when climbing Lowther Hill and Green Lowther from Leadhills or Wanlockhead. The Southern Upland Way does provide an alternative in places but following the road is a good option on a day when the weather isn't great or when introducing children to hill walking, in which case it would be advisable to use the road to return to Wanlockhead.

THE ROUTE

	Grid Ref.	Distance
1.	886 149	0

Start: Hopetoun Arms Hotel, Main St, Leadhills. Go south on Main St towards the church. Take the left fork at the church and follow rough road uphill to Leadhills railway station.

2.	887 145	½ mile

Go off to the right passing the signal box and following the track that runs alongside the railway line towards a white house.

3.	885 143	

Just beyond the white house cross the railway at the level crossing - TAKE CARE. Once over the line follow the track for about 50 yards and then turn right onto broad grassy track. Walk towards ruined mine buildings but do not continue towards the arch, go to the left towards the buildings that sit at the top of the Wilson Shaft.

4.	885 140	¾ mile

Continue beyond the buildings and follow level track through the heather. At one point the track has been washed away and a short detour is necessary to resume the track on the far side of the gully. Track is now overgrown with heather but its line can still be made out. Continue south parallel to the road on your right. Step over fence and then continue south to join the tarmac road that leads to the radar station on the summit of Lowther Hill. You can follow the road from Wanlockhead and miss out the section from Leadhills.

5.	884 132	1 ½ miles

Turn left onto radar road and follow uphill. At various points it is possible to follow the Southern Upland Way as a short cut instead of following the road as it snakes uphill. The SUW is marked out by red posts in heather.

6.	891 108	3 ½ miles

Access to the summit is denied so it is necessary to go to the left to avoid the compound. Go through gate and then join the road that runs from Lowther Hill north east via Green Trough to Green Lowther.

7.	900 120	4 ½ miles

Once again avoid the compound and descend from Green Lowther to the south east following the fence to the summit of Peden Head.

8.	905 124	5 miles

From Peden Head descend in a north westerly direction on fairly steep ground over Windy Knoll.

9.	904 138	6 miles

At the confluence of the Windgate Burn and Dun Law there is a track which leads you past a ruin and on to a dilapidated cottage known as Lowthers. Ford river (bridge doesn't make it anymore) and follow broad track out to the B7040.

10. 899 153   7 ½ miles

Turn left along the B7040 into Leadhills. Turn left in Leadhills to return to start.

11. 886 149   8 ½ miles

End: Hopetoun Arms Hotel, Leadhills.

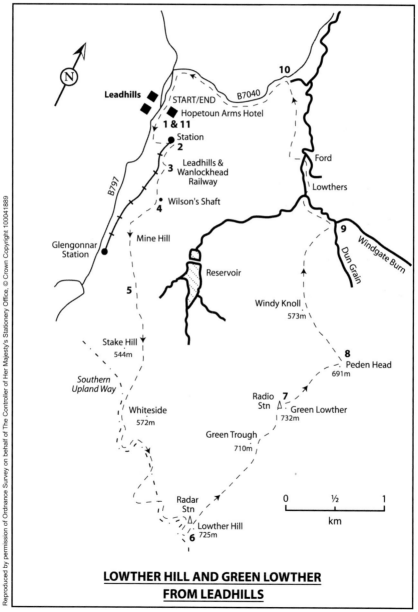

LOWTHER HILL AND GREEN LOWTHER
FROM LEADHILLS

LOWTHER HILL AND GREEN LOWTHER FROM OVER FINGLAND

Distance: 7 ½ miles.

Grade: hard.

Starting point/finishing point: Over Fingland by A702.

Maps: OS Landranger 71, OS Explorer 329. Compass required.

Terrain: open hillsides and a tarmac road closed to traffic.

BY THE WAY

The route to the summit of Lowther Hill from Over Fingland is a very different experience to the route from Leadhills. The radar station and telecom masts are still obvious on the tops but this side of the hills still retains a wildness uncompromised by an access road. Following the Southern Upland Way over three smaller hills also means a lot more effort has to go into reaching the top.

THE ROUTE

	Grid Ref.	Distance
1.	929 094	0

Start: Over Fingland, by A702. Follow the Southern Upland way uphill and cross stile. Continue to follow SUW over rather soft ground by shelter belt. Follow dyke and the SUW over Laght Hill. Continue over Comb Head and Cold Moss. SUW does not continue to summit of Lowther Hill so leave the SUW and head off to the right (north-east) to the perimeter fence of the radar compound.

2.	891 107	3 miles

Follow fence to the right and join road that goes from Lowther Hill to Green Lowther via Green Trough.

3.	901 121	4 miles

At the summit of Green Lowther go around the compound and follow the fence to Peden Head.

4.	906 124	4 ½ miles

Descend from Peden Head following the fence south east over Riccart Law Rig towards Stowgill Dod. Descend into the Riccart Cleuch to your right skirting the gully. Cross the burn to join an obvious track that takes you round to the right through a ford to a junction with another broad track.

5. 917 099   6 ½ miles

At junction with the track turn left and follow through farm at Over Fingland.

6. 929 094   7 ½ miles

End: Over Fingland, by A702..

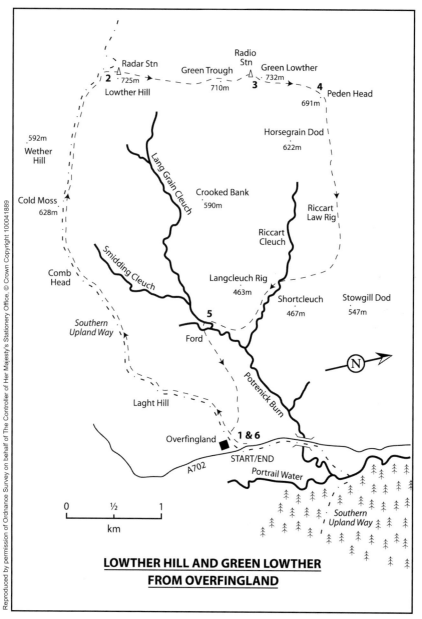

**LOWTHER HILL AND GREEN LOWTHER
FROM OVERFINGLAND**

WEDDER LAW, SCAW'D LAW, BALLENCLEUCH LAW AND ROGER LAW

Distance: 8 miles.

Grade: hard.

Starting point/finishing point: public road end, Kirkhope Farm.

Maps: OS Landranger 78, OS Explorer 329. Compass required.

Terrain: good tracks give way to very boggy ground but the hill tops are generally dry and firm.

Getting there: follow the A702 south from Elvanfoot/junction 14 M74. After about 4 miles take left signed as Daer Waterworks and follow road for 6 miles to road end.

BY THE WAY

The way to the hills is blocked by the Thick Cleuch Moss - a huge wet sponge of peat and heather out of which seeps the River Clyde and this is now regarded, somewhat controversially, to be the source of the Clyde. There are still those who believe the old couplet "Annan, Tweed and Clyde, Rise a' oot o ane hillside" which would place the source of the Clyde on Clyde Law about 5 miles to the north of Moffat.

As the going over the Thick Cleuch Moss can be very wet and very soft this walk will be best enjoyed during a hard frost or a period of drought. The hill tops however are much drier and offer views that allow you to appreciate classic Lowther Hill scenery of dark cleuchs and big doughy hills that look as if they have been turned out of jelly moulds.

The descent from Rodger Law follows Watchman's Brae so called because it is likely that a lookout would have been sited here while a conventicle was taking place during the Killing Times.

THE ROUTE

	Grid Ref.	Distance
1.	964 056	0

Start: public road end, Kirkhope Farm. Walk towards Kirkhope Farm Follow track through Kirkhope Farm and then off to the left over a wooden bridge. Follow good track up the valley of the Daer Water. Shortly after you've past Daerhead, away to your left, and at a point where the track ahead goes steeply towards a gate and the butts beyond, leave the track to the left. The path is indistinct as it follows the Thick Cleuch Burn upstream and beyond it to low point between Gana Hill and Wedder Law.

2.   941 018   3 miles

When you encounter the fence turn to the right following the fence uphill to the summit of Wedder Law.

3.   939 024   3 ½ miles

Follow the fence downhill on the west side of Wedder Law. Drift away from the fence aiming for the highest ground between Wedder Law and Scaw'd Law. Follow dyke and line of butts to the summit of Scaw'd Law.

4.   923 034   4 ¾ miles

Follow the dyke north until it meets a fence. Follow the fence to the north east and follow all the way to the summit of Ballencleuch Law.

5.   935 050   6 miles

Follow the fence downhill into col between Ballencleuch and Roger Law. Leave the fence at the col and follow a grassy track to the summit trig point on Roger Law.

6.   945 058   6 ¾ miles

Descend to the east on Watchman's Brae all the way to the road.

7.   964 056   8 miles

End: public road end, Kirkhope Farm.

The Kettletonhead Bothy

DAER TO DURISDEER AND DURISDEER TO DAER

Distance: 16 miles.

Grade: hard.

Starting point/finishing point: Daer Dam.

Maps: OS Landranger 78, OS Explorer 329. Compass required.

Terrain: the very quiet reservoir road for the first few miles is replaced by rough tracks and then by rough hillside that can be very boggy in places. The descent by the Tansley Burn can be quite trying but once it's over there are good dry tracks the whole way back.

Getting there: see Wedder Law route

BY THE WAY

Although possible in a day this walk might be better enjoyed if spread over two days and the Kettletonhead Bothy is perfectly situated to facilitate an overnight. This walk follows the same route over the Thick Cleuch Moss (source of the Clyde) as the Wedder Hill walk but continues over the watershed into Nithsdale. It is once in Nithsdale that the quality of this walk increases. The walking is on good tracks among the classic Lowther scenery that is described in the preceding route.

Durisdeer is a picturesque hamlet dominated by its grand parish church. The church is the burial place of the 2nd Duke of Queensbury and his duchess. Their mausoleum is an ornate marble wonder and doubly so because it is so unexpected in such a quiet corner of the Lowthers.

Beyond Durisdeer the route follows a Roman road in the shadow of Black Hill which seems huge despite being only just over 500 metres high. Following the Roman road means that you take in the roman fortlet from which the Romans would have controlled the pass ensuring safe passage of their troops on their way to and from their much larger fort at Crawford.

Unfortunately this circular walk has to follow the A702 for a short section, however the A702 is quiet south of Elvanfoot and the Southern Upland Way also follows the road for a time.

THE ROUTE

	Grid Ref.	Distance
1.	973 097	0

Start: Daer dam.Follow reservoir road south all the way to Kirkhope Farm.

2.	964 054	3 miles

Follow track through Kirkhope Farm and then off to the left over a wooden bridge. Follow good track up the valley of the Daer Water. Shortly after you've passed Daerhead, away to your left, and at a point where the track ahead goes steeply towards a gate and the butts beyond leave the track to the left. The path is indistinct as it follows the Thick Cleuch Burn upstream and beyond it to the low point between Gana Hill and Wedder Law.

3.	939 024	6 miles

Continue beyond the fence and follow a semblance of a track that descends with the Tansley Burn in a steep sided but shallow cleuch.

4.	924 008	7 miles

Eventually you emerge into a boat shaped valley and almost immediately you encounter a track running south to north. Turn right onto the track (north) and follow track around the base of the hillside.

5.	918 014	7 ¾ miles

At a junction of tracks where the track on the right goes very steeply uphill turn left. After 400 yards continue past the track that joins from the left. Follow track round to the right past dilapidated cottage. After about another 500 yards you encounter Kettletonhead bothy.

5.	912 021	8 ½ miles

From bothy continue north and descend through Glenaggart on a very good track. Emerge from hills into fields and continue following track which is now lined by stone dykes to minor road by the cemetery.

6. 895 036

Turn right onto road and follow into Durisdeer. In Durisdeer go to the right of the War Memorial and follow lane (dead end) that goes past the church on the right. Beyond cottages continue through gate and follow good track.

7. 898 046   9 miles

A prominent stile crosses the high dyke on the left. **EITHER** cross the stile and follow the track on the other side to a Roman fortlet. The path that continues north from the fortlet is boggy and indistinct before it joins the main track once again near the top of the pass **OR** continue straight on and view the fortlet from a distance.

8. 926 080   11 miles

Follow the track downhill on the far side and on to isolated conifer plantation (do not go towards sheepfolds) and follow track up the left hand side of the plantation out to the A702. Turn right and follow the A702 past Over Fingland. At Over Fingland you join up with the Southern Upland Way.

9. 933 102   12 ½ miles

About 400 yards beyond Over Fingland follow the SUW over the fence and away from the road to follow the burn to the footbridge over the Portrail Water.

10. 939 103   12 ¾ miles

Cross the Portrail Water and continue to follow SUW footpath through the trees and then a forestry road which crosses open country for a while before entering another plantation.

11. 962 092   15 miles

After 1 mile in the second plantation you emerge at the starting point.

12. 973 097   16 miles

End: Daer dam.

War memorial and church Durisdeer.

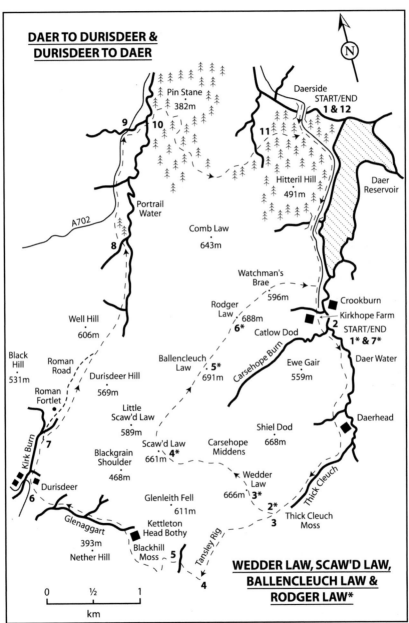

DAER TO DURISDEER & DURISDEER TO DAER

N

Pin Stane
382m

9   10

11

Daerside
START/END
1 & 12

Hitteril Hill
491m

Daer
Reservoir

Portrail
Water

A702

8

Comb Law
643m

Watchman's
Brae
596m

Rodger
Law   688m
6*

Catlow Dod

Crookburn

Kirkhope Farm
2
START/END
1* & 7*

Well Hill
606m

Ballencleuch
Law   5*
691m

Carsehope Burn

Ewe Gair
559m

Daer Water

Black
Hill
531m

Roman
Road

Durisdeer Hill
569m

Roman
Fortlet

Little
Scaw'd Law
589m

Daerhead

Kirk Burn

7

Blackgrain
Shoulder
468m

Scaw'd Law
661m   4*

Carsehope
Middens

Shiel Dod
668m

Durisdeer

6

Glenleith Fell
611m

Glenaggart

Kettleton
Head Bothy

393m
Nether Hill

Blackhill
Moss   5

Wedder
Law
666m 3*

2*

3

Thick Cleuch
Moss

Thick Cleuch

Tansley Rig

4

0   ½   1

km

WEDDER LAW, SCAW'D LAW, BALLENCLEUCH LAW & RODGER LAW*

LIGHT.
EFFICIENT.
AN EVOLUTIONARY LEAP FORWARD.

LIKE OUR GEAR.

YOU CAN LEARN A LOT FROM A FEATHER.

GoLiTe

PACKS ○ SHELTERS ○ SLEEP SYSTEMS ○ FUNCTIONAL CLOTHING   golite.co.uk ○ 0031 33 489 3179

NOTES

NOTES